Island Wise

BROADWAY BOOKS   NEW YORK

LESSONS IN LIVING FROM
THE ISLANDS OF THE WORLD

Island Wise

Janis Frawley-Holler

BROADWAY

PRINTED IN THE UNITED STATES OF AMERICA

BROADWAY BOOKS and its logo, a letter B bisected on the diagonal,
are trademarks of Random House, Inc.

Visit our website at www.broadwaybooks.com

First edition published 2003

Book design by Ellen Cipriano

Cataloging-in-Publication Data is on file with the Library of Congress.

ISBN 0-7679-1204-7

1 3 5 7 9 10 8 6 4 2

To my island guy, Darrel Holler,
for his heart full of
love, support, and encouragement

To cleave that sea in the gentle autumnal season, murmuring the name of each islet, is to my mind the joy most apt to transport the heart of man into paradise.

—NIKOS

Contents

Contents

Contents

Introduction

It is easy to fall under the spell of islands. They possess powers to heal us when our spirits seem frayed and our bodies feel battered. We dream of their slower pace of life, seek their simplicity, and covet their protective surrounding waters which isolate us from the frenzy of "mainland mania." Islands welcome us with fresh clean air, liberate our souls with their insouciance, entice us to think differently. They whisper lessons to us—to slow down, to rest, to rediscover ourselves.

When we hear the call of islands, we trade in drab business suits for brilliant, free-flowing pareos, swap Bruno Magli loafers for a pair of flip-flops, and hook a red hibiscus behind our ear. We take time to watch Matisse-bright sunsets melt into oceans, to follow butterflies through rainforests, and to inhale sea breezes tinged with the essence of the wild strawberries of northerly islands, spicy nutmeg of the West Indies, or the sweet scents of South Seas frangipani. We sip Mai Tais instead of martinis, sleep like babies the whole night through, and dare to go bare on secluded beaches. Our spirits are freed; our lives feel more fun. We give in to "island time," one of the world's greatest luxuries.

The encircling waters of islands seduce us to frequent beach bars and restaurants with soothing views of the sea. We jog along the high-tide mark instead of running to nowhere on a treadmill and float upon the surfaces of oceans as if we are one with the troughs and crests of gentle waves. Time is leisurely spent combing beaches for sea-born treasures like snowy white sand dollars, whorling moonsnails, and frosty beach glass. And, oh, the taste of morning-caught fish! Could we ever be landlocked again?

These enchanting worlds, which captivate visitors, have their roots beneath the island aura, in the reality of island life seldom savored by tourists. This life force has evolved and survived over eons of being cut off from—and virtually forgotten by—the rest of the world. Each island was alone, writing its own history and creating unique traditions, beliefs, and ways of living in harmony with the land and sea. The results have an uncanny ability to resurrect our basic instinct for a simpler, uncomplicated lifestyle, an unwavering sense of community, old-fashioned values, and a delicious, relaxed flow of life.

This island spirit was born of the earliest native islanders who were tied to the soul-inspiring beauty of these little worlds caressed by seas. It's a spirit that has been passed down through generations—both by those who came with a mind to conquer or in search of anonymity, adventure, opportunity, and religious or political freedom; and by those who were brought against their will such as slaves from Africa, shipwreck survivors, and castaways of all kinds.

They all learned to live simply, with a focus on survival. The oceans became their breadbaskets, the indigenous plants their medicines, the natural resources their shelters. They learned to take things in stride, for nothing happens quickly on islands. They became masters of innovation and creativity, for supply ships, if any, were few and far between.

The traditions of the island natives' homelands melded with the limiting conditions of their islands. New cultures were born. Languages meshed into lilting rhythms. Music delivered novel beats. An unrivaled sense of community, with all of its honorable attributes, was fathered and still flourishes. The earliest islanders have left a legacy where honesty remains honored, elders and their wisdom are still held in high esteem, and strong convictions continue to guide their actions.

Island life is not "simpleminded living." Rather it boasts the good sense to live simply, deliberately, and unencumbered by unnecessary things. It embraces a strong belief in "taking time" to do what's important for the moment instead of "time taking" us swiftly down sandy roads we don't want to travel.

So islanders take time to cook from scratch and relish the clean flavors as a family, to walk or ride bikes whenever they have the chance, and to hang clothes to dry in the trade winds so bed linens smell like sunshine and fresh air. They take time to care for their own children and parents, to linger on porches and chat with friends, to squeeze just-picked oranges into juice and turn berries into homemade jam. Their philosophy is succinctly summed up by the popular Hawaiian hand signal for "hang loose." The world knows it as living on "island time."

So come along and discover the inner soul of the earth's islands. Take time to hear its whispers; take time to heed its wisdom. For, as the essays in this book will show, the island spirit is simply a glorious state of mind—the "island wise" way of thinking—which can make life feel sweeter, wherever we are.

Island Wise

Set Your Clock
to Island Time

Those of us struck by island fever yearn to live on island time—
those delectable, unhurried days where even the surf seems to
drift effortlessly ashore and those long arching fronds of coconut
palms sway in a slow, sensual dance on the mildest of sea breezes.
We fantasize about living as islanders do, envying their light and
leisurely approach to each day, their patience with themselves,
others, and the world in general.

   Living on island time is something we envy because, in our
mainland worlds, we travel at a dizzying pace, determined to
keep up with the pack; we rush through stress-filled, jam-packed
schedules with no thought of pausing to appreciate the quietly
magical details of our lives. The whispers of our inner voice go
unheeded, yet leave us with a gnawing sense that life is not meant
to be lived as a race against time. So we are drawn to islands—

those perfect spots that give us permission to drop out, slow down, and rejuvenate to their patient, waltzing rhythm.

Island time is the very soul of island life. From the hot, steamy jungles of Borneo to the snow-capped mountainous isles of Alaska's Inside Passage, islanders know how to live in step with their own innate tempo—a pace that fosters an ease of attitude, a warm feeling about life, a knack for delighting in simple plea-sures, and time to tarry in precious places with cherished people. They see no merit in living weighted down by anxiety, urgency, and stress, for they learned long ago the lesson of Aesop's Tor-toise and the Hare fable: "Slow and steady wins."

My husband says I'm a "steadfast tortoise," a name I relish because being an island-style woman blesses me with inclinations to linger and appreciate the good all around me, to stop and think things through and stay true to who I am.

When we visited the isle of Crete, one of my personal goals was to hike the Samariá Gorge, the longest gorge in Europe. In the darkness of early morning, we boarded a tour bus filled with Germans and Scandinavians for the long ride up into the moun-tains as the trail (which takes six to seven hours to hike) steeply descends from the peaks of the White Mountains down to the Libyan Sea.

The minute we got off the bus—*swoooooosh!*—the other hik-ers were off at such a manic clip that they left us, literally, in their dust. We walked on slowly because, looking up at the magical beauty of the mountains in the colors of dawn, we were struck with awe. It was a sight I doubt any of the other travelers had even noticed.

"If we don't speed up a bit," Darrel said after a while, "I'm afraid we'll miss the boat back to our hotel."

It was difficult, however, to speed up because with every few steps there was more and more beauty to relish: hot pink oleanders growing in the wild, Cretan "forest rangers" descending the trail on donkeys, ruins of ancient villages poised along banks of peaceful streams. We snapped pictures of artsy afternoon shadows on the rocky sides of cliffs and zigzagged across rushing waters atop massive boulders. The gorge was a never-ending masterpiece of more natural beauty than we had ever imagined, and we took the time to savor every new marvel.

And the hikers? It's a funny thing. We caught up with them each time they stopped for a cigarette break and passed them by so many times throughout the hike that I lost count. It was truly a day of the Tortoise and the Hare, for after seven hours of steady progress, we "tortoises" were among the first to arrive at the sea where the boat awaited. Our prize for hiking on island time was a treasured collection of memories highlighting some of Mother Nature's best works, lots of photos to add to our ever-growing scrapbook, and much healthier lungs!

Living on island time doesn't require us to pack up and move to our own most beloved isle. It's so much easier than that, for no matter where we live, we can simply choose to slow down and relish life. It's important to realize that this way of being doesn't encompass a lazy lifestyle, nor does it breed irresponsibility. Island time is simply about eliminating haste, chewing slowly to appreciate tastes, avoiding "too-timers" (too much TV, too many too-long phone calls, too much obsessing about work, etc.), and it's never ever equating time with "pressure." It is recognizing that time isn't the traitor of our day—the true archenemy is how we view the seconds, schedule the minutes, and live the hours. It's realizing that time can, indeed, be on our side, just by taking a deep breath and believing that the "time of your life" is truly a gift to be used in an island-wise way.

When we begin to break old habits of sprinting through life, it feels awkward, even foreign, at first. After a particularly harried few months, I sought solace in the serene aura of Paradise Island in the Bahamas. Yet after three days of doing nothing but yoga and taking long walks on the beach, I found myself feeling very emotional and off balance. I happened to run into a yogi who gave me an explanation:

"Think of yourself as a child's top spinning at such a high rate of speed every moment of the day that it's impossible to stay connected with yourself—with who you are and what you truly want. When the top begins to slow down, it starts to wobble. The slower it goes, the greater the wobble, until it breathes a sigh of relief and settles into its resting place. It's the eventual discovery of this peaceful place which is the ultimate gift of slowing down."

Island Wise

As you begin to find your own island-wise way of being, remember that setting your clock to island time is the most important step. It is the universal prescription that comes from all healing islands, from the Caribbean to the South China Sea. Living at a slower pace changes us. We're able to think logically and independently, remember our manners, distinguish right from wrong, and realize what is truly important in life. Slowing down allows us to go with the flow of life rather than always feeling as though we're swimming upstream. On island time we adopt the words of islander William Shakespeare as our model: "Wisely and slow; they stumble that run fast."

Taha'a, the Tahitian Islands

ADOPT NATURAL PLEASURES

*I*t's impossible to get up on the wrong side of the bed when you awaken each morning in a Garden of Eden encircled by a lagoon of calm waters graduating in color from a rich deep blue to a shimmering opal as it shallows up to the shore. The island's homesteads rest, relaxed and quiet, between the lagoon and the peaks and valleys of the mountains towering over it all in majestic green.

Curtains of bright colors float on the breeze, in and out of the unscreened window openings of the modest homes that look out to yards so stunning they could be mistaken for botanical gardens. They're overabundant in the natural beauty of ultra-tropical trees—banana (of all kinds), breadfruit, mango, papaya, avocado, and grapefruit—and of flowers and shrubs ablaze in color—red and pastel pink gingers, multicolored crotons, snow-white gardenias, deep-pink frangipani, and every other tropical flower you can imagine. It's a vision, the kind we all fantasize about; it's Taha'a, an off-the-beaten-path island of Tahiti, shaped just like a hibiscus flower.

Edwin and his wife Jacqueline welcomed me, eager to share the best of their island's ways. He was playing a ukulele and singing a dreamy South Seas tune, decked out in freshly picked flowers woven into a crown around his head, a necklace of local shells hand carved into a big, bold chiefly design, and a colorful floor-length pareo wrapped and tied beneath his belly. Jacqueline, whose hat was encircled in a woven band of extra-fragrant double gardenias and deep-pink and pale-yellow lantanas, wore a brilliant blue-and-yellow-flowered floor-length dress.

Their four-wheel-drive was prettied up with flowers, too—a string of gardenias lined the dashboard and flowers were braided up the support braces of the canopy that shaded the back seating. Jacqueline offered me a snow-white tiare, the flower of Tahiti, to tuck behind my left ear (the married ear), which made me feel as special as a little girl playing dress up. Its natural, soft scent blessed me, and soothed me, for the rest of the day.

"The one thing you'll discover," an Australian who married into a Taha'an family said, "is that the people love to surround themselves in beauty and color every moment of the day. They look to nature to do that."

We were off, traveling a carless road that wound into the mountains, surrounded the whole way in tropical fantasy: forests abloom in hundreds of flowers of brilliant hues and the marvelous shapes of the gigantic leaves of heliconia, elephant ears, and white birds of paradise—tropically lush in their climb up the slopes. Cows and horses lazily grazed near rushing streams winding through coconut plantations; outriggers lay idle in the lagoon below, and, beyond, the thatched-roof huts of the black-pearl farmers stood guardian over the water.

When we stopped way up high near a mountaintop, it was a South Seas dream come alive: young men and women, clad in brilliant pareos and adorned in flowers (worn as crowns, leis, or tucked in their hair) sliced fresh papaya, mango, and green grapefruit, which they arranged with tiny bananas on trays artfully covered in folded banana leaves accented in red hibiscus. It was a scene that would have inspired Paul Gauguin to take out his brushes and paint the day away.

The men opened green coconuts with one island-style blow of their machetes, whacking off the tops to offer refreshing drinks of coconut water; then they opened the ripe coconuts, quickly grating the fresh sweet meat against a stick stuck in the ground. The girls sprinkled it over the papaya, made neat little mounds next to the bananas, and encouraged me to follow their lead. I broke off bite-sized pieces of the nutty-flavored bananas, pushed them into the coconut, popped them into my mouth, and smiled at the blending flavors.

Edwin grinned and strummed his ukulele, a woman with long dark hair danced, her swaying Tahitian hips and graceful hands signing out the stories of the ancient songs the young people sang. When the day was over, a girl put her lei around my neck, another put her crown of flowers on my head. I've seldom felt so special, prettied up in flowers and sharing the spirit of these hard-working, yet happy-go-lucky islanders who continually adorn their world in Mother Nature's most artistic treasures.

IT'S OUR NATURE

We sweeten up our life when we invite the simple beauty of nature into the intimacy of our homes and our personal spaces. It isn't difficult, nor does it take a lot of time, talent, or money. Just think natural—a single daisy in a bud vase, fresh herbs growing on a kitchen windowsill, a seashell as a soap dish, a sweetgrass basket overflowing in pineapples, mangoes, and apples adorning the dining room table, a natural sponge to trickle water over our body when we bathe, a wreath of deep-red chili peppers hanging on a kitchen wall. These are the thing that enhance our lives in the most positive of Taha'an ways; and these inexpensive practices energize the essence of our surroundings.

Native peoples have long had an enviable union with all of the offsprings of Mother Nature, acknowledging that each and every thing possesses a spirit, whether it be a thousand-year-old redwood tree or a honey bee. They have always acknowledged the interdependence of every single thing within nature. They respect nature, they learn from it, they lean on it. It's an innate element of their own spirit, of their beliefs; it's an important dimension of their protocol which directs morality and demeanor.

Children, too, naturally relish the comfort of the natural world. They're always eager to welcome nature by putting frogs in their pockets and fireflies in jars; by gathering wildflowers, collecting rocks, enjoying the warm, squishy feel of mud and the grounding power of handfuls of earth; and by finding solace climbing trees when they want to be alone to sort things out. As adults, we find it easy to forget how much simple, natural pleasures add to our lives.

So open the curtains, pull up the blinds, and let the sunny warmth of life into your homes and offices. Look out; look up. Take in the blueness of sky and its vastness, a symbol of infinite possibilities; look to the trees for consolation and strength and to the feathers of birds for a lighter attitude toward life. Set out natural wooden bowls of nuts in their earthy-toned protective shells as reminders to safeguard what's important to us, whether it be our children or our environment.

Scatter seashells around your rooms; they epitomize the importance of a strong, stable home, a sanctuary where we can simply be ourselves to laugh, play, love, and rest in safety. Seek the raw beauty of driftwood, so gracefully sculpted by just going with the flow of the sea, a suggestion to let things happen in their own time. Set aside time for sunsets, for the gorgeousness of each one is a daily sign that endings can, indeed, be new beginnings in disguise.

And then there are flowers. The famous impressionist Claude Monet once said, "More than anything, I must have flowers, always, always."

Fresh flowers, whether they grace a living room or bloom in our gardens, are healing. Their beauty is unsurpassed and they act as the supreme mood changer, chasing away the blues, perking us up when we're ill, adding a cheery sentiment to a regular day. They make us feel special, even if we give them to ourselves, for they've long been linked to love. We get married donned in flowers, we commemorate special occasions with them, and we return to the earth surrounded by them.

It's important to cultivate a relationship with the beauty Mother Nature provides, for without it, our spirits begin to wilt. It keeps us connected with the soul of the earth, it sets our moods swaying, it enriches our own private little worlds. As Madame Marie Curie said, "All my life through, the new sights of nature made me rejoice like a child."

✸ *Be a flower child.* The next time you have a chance to dress up, remember that there's nothing as elegant as a woman with an orchid tucked behind her ear, or a man with a fresh carnation in his lapel. Many little blossoms can be woven into chokers, made into bracelets to adorn your wrist or ankle or, for the ultimate, make an armband of little cascading orchids. A creative florist will be brimming over with ideas that can make you look Taha'an beautiful.

✸ *Seek the healing power of natural settings.* Walk through the woods, listen to the owls, follow the paths of dragonflies, sit on a hilltop and try to reach the stars, immerse yourself in the shapes of clouds, or head to the mountains and make a snowball in July. Dust off your watercolors and paint your own garden; plant a tree or go beachcombing.

✸ *Water power.* Float off into island-style relaxation watching tropical fish drift by in an office aquarium, set flowers afloat in your bathwater, place a Zen-sounding waterfall near your bed to lull you deep into sleep, open the windows and listen to the rain, seek the ocean, or dangle your feet in the cool waters of a cleansing creek.

13

✭ *Don't forget that fire is part of nature, too.* Darken the room and set aglow candles of every height and in every possible space, or stretch out in front of a crackling, cheery fire on a cozy winter night.

Nassau, the Bahamas

TAKE BACK YOUR "SUN"DAYS

*N*assau, the capital of the Bahamas, hums along to its own goombay rhythms during the week, from the hustling vendors of the straw market to the conchmen of Potters Cay who dice up tangy salads made of queen conchs so fresh they're still dripping in seawater. Interisland ferries are coming and going with all kinds of island cargo, from those sweet Bahamian pineapples to luscious crawfish. World-class yachts make their way in and out of the harbor, and horse-drawn fringe-topped surreys carry tourists through the historic narrow lanes of

Old Nassau, resplendent in pastel-pink colonial government buildings and rousing in lingering old spirits like that of Blackbeard, who once loved to wreak havoc along the wharf.

When Sunday morning rolls around, however, the whole feel of the island changes, and the quiet, peaceful glow of early morning seems to last all day long. It's a memorable picture: the rising sun gives a golden cast to the waters where traditional working sailboats lie lazily at anchor amid reflections of lofty trees growing along the shoreline. The roads are quiet, barren of traffic, and businesses are closed up tight.

The Bahamas is an island nation that has chosen to uphold what once was a universal custom, if not a law of spirit—honoring Sundays. The islanders still celebrate the seventh day of the week as a time to express their spirituality, rest their bodies, grant their minds a much needed respite, and nurture relationships with loved ones. Tragically, too much of the mainland has deemed our need for just one day a week to revive our outlook on life as unimportant. Instead of a day of rest, it has become just another day in a long, active, hectic week.

But the Bahamians embrace their Sunday tradition—it's something they look forward to all week long. The preparations usually begin on Saturday: cleaning house, washing clothes, hanging them in the warm sun to dry, shopping, running errands, and getting a head start on cooking up traditional foods like johnnycake, chicken souse, and guava duff. It's all in preparation for

Sunday feasting: healthy Bahamian family breakfasts and dinners fit for the Queen.

Early Sunday mornings are my favorite time in Nassau. I love standing beneath a casuarina tree growing along the shoreline, watching as families leisurely stroll the waterfront on their way to church. Each member is dressed to the nines in his or her Sunday best: the young boys sport smiles, snow-white starch-crisp shirts, and perfectly creased black trousers; the little girls are dolled up in frilly dresses, their plaited hair bejeweled in colorful beads; the women wear dresses the colors of rainbows, accented by the chicest of hats; the men wear impeccably pressed suits and ties in spite of the steadily rising temperature.

The cathedral fills up quickly, both with locals and tourists of all faiths, as everyone who comes to the island quickly discovers that church back home seldom feels as good as it does here. The Mass takes on the reverent vitality of a congregation that puts every ounce of its heart and soul into the expression of the beliefs each member lives by. The words of age-old hymns are perfectly paired with the soul-stirring rhythms of the island, with a tad of gospel thrown in. Everyone's spirit, including mine, soars into a wondrous, uplifting place, making life feel just too good.

Afterward, friends and extended families dally awhile to chat, then head off to gather in homes to share those big breakfasts that always begin with a blessing of the table and finish with lively, yet Bahamian-polite, conversation. The rest of the day is devoted to easy, pleasurable activities: fishing, family picnics, leisurely strolls, drives to the villages in the island countryside, or simply rocking in chairs on shaded verandahs cooled by the wind coming in off the harbor.

SUNDAY SCHOOL

We can all bring that warm, simple glow of sunny islands into our "Sun"days or whatever day of the week we choose to honor. Simply look upon the day as the springtime of each week and orchestrate it as a time of awakening, of rejuvenation for a burnt-out spirit, of rebirth for a tired body, and of reconnection with family members usually off and running in different directions. In a coconut shell, make it a day that requires you to luxuriate in island time.

Put some thought into what this day can represent in your own home. Ask your mother or grandmother how she used to define her day of rest before it became just like any other day of the week. Tap her memories for sacred rituals that can be passed on to you, then think about resurrecting them. Or invent your own new ways of making this one day of the week special, restful, and something you can look forward to.

Our Sunday activities may change throughout the different phases of our life, but that warm, mellow feel of relaxed rejuve-

nation, with no sense of urgency, no trace of stress, needs to remain constant. When I think back to the Sundays of my childhood, they were always a restful day for family. They began with
sleeping in, eating soft, warm doughnuts and crispy bacon, downtime devoted to the Sunday papers, and a late church service
where we could hardly contain our giggles as the choir's soprano
soloist came close to shattering windows. Then we all piled into
the car for a long drive that relaxed my very hard-working dad.
Our Midwest winter rides were to neighboring towns for an afternoon movie and dinner at a favorite restaurant; summer jour-
neys were through the country, sometimes even to neighboring
states for a treat like real Tennessee barbecue, or to a pool-and-
picnic area in Missouri. Chores and homework had to be done by
Saturday evening so we all could bask in rest and relaxation on
Sunday. It was the "rule"—a rule much more meaningful and
treasured to me now as an adult looking back.

When I went away to a Florida college, I held on to sleeping
late, lounging on the beach, playing a game of tennis, enjoying a
good Sunday supper, and, of course, making a call home to check
in with my family. When I married, it became a day of sailing
with picnic fixings, plenty of pillows, Jimmy Buffett tapes, and a
windsurfer on board. Sunday rituals change with time, yet all are
reflections of my parents' message about the purpose of Sundays
and what they can bring to our lives.

Honoring Sundays seems to have come much more naturally

for mainland worlds of another era, before malls stayed open on Sundays and families became so scattered. For many of those who live on the healing islands of the world, like the Bahamas, celebrating Sundays is as second nature as brushing their teeth. It's a part of their spiritual heritage, handed down from one generation to another. Thank goodness we have them to remind us to honor that part of our being that needs rest and rebirth every seven days. The Bahamian people are a wonderful example for us to follow.

In the beginning, break old habits by setting up guidelines based on the three *r*'s of island-style Sundays: rest, relaxation, and recreation, the perfect Bahamian prescription for health and happiness. Plan activities that only fall under these headings so that come Monday morning, you arise with a fresh outlook on the week. Avoid anything complicated and give in to simple whims: sway on a porch swing, stroll in the park, work on your tan. Play games with the kids, laze away a few hours fishing, engage in a game of checkers with your father. A step at a time leads to Sundays that will feel like mini-vacations to your favorite island.

☆ *Put "Sun"day on the calendar.* Put intent into the day by blocking out each and every Sunday (or whatever day you choose) on your calendar as a day for yourself and/or your family, even if you have to think of it as a scheduled appointment that, no matter what crops up, you just can't break.

* *Make it a "no-day."* No work, no housework, no errands, no shopping, no laundry, and no paying bills. Get the work, the chores, the running around, the cooking, and, yes, the homework, done and out of the way by Saturday evening; never allow a Sunday to be "catch-up day."

* *Turn off the alarm clock.* Allow yourself a Sunday awakening that's easy, slow, and on your own, in lieu of being jolted out of a blissful sleep by an alarm clock. It's a morning for an indulgent beginning like having breakfast in bed or outside on the patio, or a royally late brunch somewhere special. Linger over cups of hot tea, the morning paper, a just-blooming flower in the garden, or the feel of a favorite recliner.

* *Stir your soul.* If you haven't taken advantage of many faiths' Saturday evening services, you may want to attend a church, synagogue, temple, or mosque; but do it with Bahamian flair—dress up to show it's a celebration of spirit. Or maybe you simply want to write in a gratitude journal, or say prayers or affirmations on the banks of a river, the top of a mountain, or in a backyard treehouse. Make it a Sunday of services that speak to your soul.

Sark, the Channel Islands, United Kingdom

✺

DEFY THE MAINLAND

Some say that time just passed on by the Isle of Sark without even a glance. My theory is that when time came a-knocking, the independent Sarkese simply slammed the door in its face.

"We're so happy with our own little way of life here," a Sarkese said, "we wouldn't want it any other way."

So if people come calling and try to change things, they just tell them, "Well, there's a boat leaving tomorrow." The islanders simply want no part of the pace, pollution, or problems that progress and modern development bring.

Everything about this soul-caressing pocket of a maritime, countryside paradise—a mere three by one and a half miles in size—is positively unique. Sitting 350 feet above sea level, its rocky cliffs boast forty miles of craggy coastline. On most days, the Normandy coast of France is in view (the old stone homes, as well as the bays, have French names), yet the Sarkese are loyal to the Crown of England eighty miles away. But don't call them English—they're Sarkese and that's that.

As the smallest independent feudal state in Europe, the isle remains governed by the Seigneur of Sark (lord of the island) along with the Chief Pleas, the island's parliament, made up of one representative for every 10 of the 589 residents. Many of its laws—such as the illegality of divorce as well as of motor cars, airplanes, helicopters, and anything else that produces noise and exhaust fumes (except a few tractors confined to the farms); the 10 P.M. to 6 A.M. curfew; and the decree that all able-bodied men rotate duty as constable—are rooted in the island's magical other-era feel that speaks directly to the simple soul of the good life.

It all started in 1565 when Helier de Carteret, the Seigneur of St. Ouen in the nearby isle of Jersey, leased the island from Queen Elizabeth I. He landed with forty families, dividing it into the forty tenements which still exist today, the majority owned by descendants of true original settlers. The most famous of a long line of Seigneurs was Dame Sibyl Hathaway, a courageous, strong, yet considerate leader who, during World War II, stood up to the Germans when they invaded with the intent to evacuate the islanders and occupy the strategically placed isle. She and her people refused to leave their land.

During the five-year occupation, they were robbed of their individualistic way of life and suffered great hardship. On May 7, 1945, the Germans unconditionally surrendered to the Allies. The next day, when Churchill broadcast that the war was over, Dame Sibyl defiantly celebrated in the presence of the German soldiers by raising the Union Jack, holding a dance, lighting a bonfire, and defying the German curfew. The neighboring islands of Guernsey and Jersey were liberated on May 9, although the Sarkese continued to live in terror as the occupying Germans were determined to defend the Isle of Sark "down to the last man." The islanders were finally freed on the afternoon of May 10, when once again their independent nature was unleashed stronger than ever. The indomitable spirit of Dame Sibyl lives on in the islanders who rallied behind her until her death in 1976. Some locals believe she inspired the confidence felt on the isle to this day—the courage of conviction, the great pride of heritage, and the admirable determination to keep Sark being Sark.

I salute the independent islanders for their strong commitment to their enviable quality of life. The island itself is a supreme "leveler" of the ego: "incomers" arrive to escape the trappings of other places; there's no superstar culture, no status symbols, no keeping-up-with-the-Joneses mentality and, thus, very little envy or jealousy. This absence promotes a more cohesive spirit and a close-knit community. Traditional values reign, and the isle's heart beats to a strong, honest work ethic as well as a collective conscience to protect the island's pastoral beauty. It's all enhanced by Sark's famous purity of air and resulting clarity of light, which draw artists and photographers from around the world to capture the dramatic land- and seascapes.

These earthly treasures, along with an old-world aura, encourage all to take daily communion with nature: sneaking off down secret little paths into the green smells of woodlands whose clear streams trickle through valleys; cherishing sights of children riding Shetland ponies along flowering tree-lined lanes; riding bicycles adorned with woven-reed baskets overflowing in day-brightening blossoms; listening to the nostalgic clippity-clop of horsedrawn buggies en route to the ice cream shop; and relishing meadow after meadow of long green-golden grasses swaying with the wind, overtaken in springtime by lavish patchworks of sunny-spirited wildflowers ("like the English countryside sixty years ago," a day-tripping Brit told me).

To me, the soul of Sark is its cliff walks, which provide refreshing, awe-inspiring strolls that start high atop the cliffs and follow narrow dirt paths framed in dancing grasses and hedges thick in wildflowers all the way down to the sea. Comfortable benches are placed along the way—great opportunities to relax and reflect, taking in breathtaking vistas of creamy blue-green seas and rocky outcroppings where puffins gather. It's no wonder that the favorite pastime of the islanders is to just "go out and wander."

"Rather than respect what's here," an islander said, "outsiders always want to impose foreign ways on us. The European community seems to trivialize our way of life—it doesn't fit into their perception of the modern world."

But just ask the independent Sarkese and they'll tell you that what they treasure most about their island life is that it hasn't followed the course of the modern world—and they wouldn't change that for all the tea in London.

THAT AIR OF INDEPENDENCE

"Everyone should have a little Sark air breathing inside of them," an islander told me as we shared Sark cream tea in a tea garden. "Why should we—why should anyone?—change within simply because they want us to change without?"

When we inject this kind of resolute energy into our spirit, an independent life force bursts on to the scene, piloting us to where our own true happiness lies, beckoning us to listen to our inner callings and to go for them—to break free of comfort zones and take risks—and to defy the continent, as it may be. We become Sarkese confident: bold, honest, and free in our thoughts, words, and deeds. And as the islanders have shown, it empowers authentic living.

As independent individuals we are meant to embrace common sense, to speak up when we disagree, and to never blindly follow rules or anything else. We need to always ask questions, challenge authority when our views differ, and take responsibility for our own lives, successes, and mistakes. Our intuition is finely tuned and we must learn to trust it, to stand up for what we believe in, to fight for what we think is right, and to not be easily influenced or swayed. When we do this, we are living with a Sarkese-style approach to life.

But, as we know, there are always those who want to change us—to knock the wind out of our independent sails so they can exert control over us and inflict their way of thinking, believing, and acting upon us. It happens to islands all the time—people fall in love with a place, move there, then want to change it into what they had back home, effectively ruining its rhythm, its beauty, and its spirit. And it happens to us, as individuals, all the time, too.

When we allow our independent nature to be stolen—when we betray our own feelings and rights just to keep peace, when we sell out our own priorities to give more importance to another's, when we relinquish our capability to stand up and say, "No more!"—we spiral down into dependency. We change.

Neediness becomes our master—a need to please, a need to be taken care of, a need for security, status, money, and nonaccountability. We give up thinking for ourselves, doing for ourselves, even feeling for ourselves, losing that all-important self-nurturing intimacy with our inner being, our personal dignity, our brain power. We never fully mature emotionally, intellectually, or spiritually. We lose ourselves.

Giving up our independence is like sleepwalking through life, not seeing all that life had planned to offer us as solid individuals. Our days become tainted by low self-esteem and lack of self-respect; it dams up our energy, buries our talents, and bars us from personal growth. Its side effects are devastating: depression, feelings of worthlessness, and lack of power in our own lives.

Developing a flair for independent living is really about connecting with our own inner wisdom and letting it guide our life; it's about reclaiming our freedom to live true to our own independent nature, overseen by self-respect, self-reliance, self-sufficiency, and, thus, self-preservation. We maintain reverence for our own individual beliefs and choices, yet we realize the importance of give-and-take as *equals* in relationships, within families, and as part of a team at work. For asserting independence isn't about bending others to our will, it's about making sure they don't rob us of who we are.

So join in an alliance with yourself, blooming in your own vivid spirit with the strength and beauty of the sturdy wildflowers along a cliff walk. Your life will then feel as reliable and your heart as content as that of a Sarkese wandering down an independent island path on a bright-blue spring day.

---

* *Assert yourself.* Take assertiveness training. Sign up at a college, counseling center, women's/men's resource center, or for an adult education class and watch yourself shift into a confident, independent person tasting life more fully, taking on challenges, and thinking for yourself.

* *Stand by your convictions.* Make an honest life. Uphold personal responsibility, for yourself and for your actions. Play out life as an equal, not as a submissive putting your day's decisions in another's hands; follow only the genuineness of your true spirit even when it seems daunting.

* *Set limits.* Never accept, or believe in, behavior from others that insults either your spirit or your intellect. When someone tries to degrade you, simply say to yourself (and eventually to that person), "I don't value your opinion on that subject." After repeated practice, you'll start to believe it and, thus, maintain your self-esteem and equal footing in the relationship.

★ *Curiosity never killed the cat!* Always ask "why" questions when it comes to requests, persuasive messages, authority figures, religious leaders, general beliefs and attitudes. Seek the logical; form your own thoughts and adhere to your own ethics and morals.

Prince Edward Island, Canada

HONEST TO GOODNESS

*I*f I had my way, the whole world would be like Prince Edward Island, Canada's smallest province. It has that safe, homey feel that comes from a strong sense of community, old-fashioned values, and its other-era aura where milkmen still deliver to the front door, good clean fun heads the menu of ice cream socials, and hamlets are framed in apple trees and blueberries growing wild along the roadside.

I love hopping in a car, just me and my camera, heading out to discover the pastoral land of Anne of Green Gables. It's artist-gorgeous in rolling farmlands the color of emeralds and dotted in little snow-white churches whose steeples stretch skyward; in fields dense in everything from the yellow flowers of potato vines to the sweet, golden scent of hay; and in meadows stunning in inspiring palettes of brilliant wildflowers mingling with the taller lavenders of lupins. It all sweeps across the isle right up to the cobalt-blue northern Atlantic Ocean.

Quaint little maritime villages are scattered along that coastline, too, enveloped in the wonderful character of fishing and lobster fleets and people of hearty strength who have made their living challenging a cold sea since their ancestors came ashore long ago. The air still sings in their strong accents—Irish brogues, the French of Acadians, the tongue-rolling Scotch, with a little mainland Canadian heard here and there—and in their intoxicating music—spirited foot-stomping fiddlin' tunes, moving seafaring ballads, and the haunting echos of bagpipes. The aromas sent me reeling back into my grandma's kitchen, filled with the warm smell of bread baking (often in old-fashioned wood-burning ovens) and the comforting perfume of cinnamon and nutmeg from warm oat cakes, scones, and butter tarts.

Roadside produce stands and market gardens brim with more fresh colors than a painter's album: a legion of reds from radishes to raspberries, tinges of greens from peppers and peas to zucchini and fresh herbs, the earth tones of potatoes, the rich, deep hues of blackberries, and the bright reds, yellows and oranges of nasturtiums. This potpourri of nature's incredible edibles are displayed unattended—it's self-serve, self-pay, and make your own change.

The rest of the island is just as trusting. When a friend offered to bake her special strawberry pie, we walked down the lane to a neighbor's field where we kneeled on a ground of cool red soil and hand-plucked six quarts of the biggest, juiciest strawberries I had ever seen. As I fetched my wallet, she said, "Don't worry about it. I keep track and settle up with him at the end of berry season."

A few days later I watched two islanders barter, a Prince Edward Island tradition. They agreed on a fair exchange of fresh-caught lobster for a horse collar. But most impressive of all was when a business deal was sealed with a man's word and a handshake as binding as a mainland contract.

I wandered about the island for days, driving the back roads and bicycling parts of the Confederation Trail, enjoying a liberating sense of unadulterated safety, unburdened by even the slightest hint of risk or suspicion. While lingering atop a huge sand dune, admiring the waves of the sea, I put it all together: the isle's emancipating aura is rooted in a code of behavior refreshingly based on honesty, fairness, reliability, and responsibility, and an abiding sense of morality, which allows me and other visitors to roam without worry and islanders to seldom even think about locking doors or removing keys from car ignitions. It's a quality of life I long for back home.

GIVE YOUR WORD—HONESTLY

Speaking openly and honestly is the cornerstone of Prince Edward Island's sense of safety and its venerable code of ethics. Being able to place confidence in another's word contributes to a widespread integrity that in turn forms the foundation of security within this community. Sadly, these virtues have been disinherited in many other parts of the world.

But honesty, integrity, and respect for one another are vital parts of island life where societies are small and isolated and locals so interdependent. Islanders realize that how we use words has effects and consequences, that words can instill a mutual respect and trust or, on the other hand, disdain and mistrust.

The residents of Prince Edward Island know that if they're in some sort of trouble, there will always be a helping hand because of the camaraderie evolved from their code of ethics. If a farmer's barn burns down, people will come from miles around to rebuild it quickly, for honesty in thought, word, and deed is at the core of a comforting support system. Such societies allow our souls to relax from the worry, stress, and fear of feeling alone and isolated in dealing with our problems, a feeling that many of us grapple with, despite the crowds of mainland living.

If a tire goes flat on a Prince Edward Island road, you don't have to doubt the motives of the person stopping to help. But I remember how terrified I was when my tire blew on a Florida interstate. I called AAA, but was told they couldn't reach me for an hour. When a car stopped behind me to help out, I didn't know whether I should be thankful or scared, but fright took over as I hesitated to roll down my window to speak to him. I was suspicious of his intention, a reflection, not on him, but of the society we live in. Within seconds a State Trooper arrived who worked with my Good Samaritan to get me on my way.

Unfortunately, in today's mainland worlds, most of us feel that we simply can't count on the integrity of a man's word—or the man, even when it comes to our country's leaders, the attorneys on which our judicial system relies, religious leaders, advertisers with their scripts of persuasion, and on and on. Misrepresentation and outright lying are so prevalent that, unlike islanders, we have come to expect it and, even more disturbing, accept it.

Without realizing it, we begin to throw words around like politicians—with little thought to their meaning, to their effects, to their consequences. Breaking our word becomes commonplace. We often resort to "easy words" that only serve to appease in the moment, "snow words" aimed to pull the wool over another's eyes, and "my way words" used to get our own way no matter what.

It's a dangerous thing to get a reputation for speaking dishonestly. Thomas Jefferson warned of the self-defeating web a single lie can weave: "He who permits himself to tell a lie once, finds it much easier to do it a second and third time, till at length it becomes habitual; he tells lies without attending to it, and truths without the world's believing him. This falsehood of the tongue leads to that of the heart, and in time deprives all its good disposition."

Make sure that doesn't happen to you. And always remember the words of Alexander Pope: "An honest man's the noblest work of God."

---

* *Keep Your Promises.* Promises are pledges, not only of words and actions to be taken, but of our character. They're presents not to be given lightly, never to be taken back, and never to be broken, for when they are, real damage can be done. Make promises only when you're sure that you can follow through with them—you'll feel lighter and more at peace.

* *Be word-wise.* Each and every word we speak affects someone in some way. Words can create happiness, laughter, delight, security, reliability, and respect, or they can denigrate, cause disappointment, mistrust, sadness, tears, or knock someone else's self-esteem right down the tubes. Think about what effect you

hope to achieve, then choose words that will invite positive results.

✭ *Eliminate "easy words."* When we're rushing out the door or caught in a spot, "easy words" can easily get out of hand. If there isn't enough time to process the situation, postpone your response until later. Handle the situation with honor, saying, "I really owe it to you to make sure I can commit to this before I give you my word. We'll discuss it tonight."

✭ *Heed word warnings.* Tune in to and live by the signals your inner being sends. Diminished breathing, throat tightening, voice sounding pinched, louder, or soaring into the next octave are all signs of inward discomfort with what we have chosen to say. Realize that when we "speak our peace," everything just flows.

Anegada, the British Virgin Islands

BE IN THE QUIET

negada is a gentler world, astonishingly quiet and divinely peaceful. As flat as a delicious crepe and sitting low in the water, it's often mistaken for a mystical mirage surfacing at the remote, far northern edge of the British Virgin Islands. The gorgeous Caribbean lobster-bearing reef embracing the island grows skyward in shallow water, rendering it dangerous to boats (three hundred wrecks lie offshore) and protectively keeping the world at bay. The isle's interior is home to seventy bright-pink flamingos that live unharassed in a huge, muddy pond; children run fancy-free, island cows (which are shared communally among the two hundred locals) roam at their will, and the morning cock-a-doodle-dos of laid-back roosters sound as though they've been sedated.

There's not much to do, yet along the island's coastline of dreamy bays and deserted beaches there's time and space for everything you've ever dreamt of doing. The warm golden-sand beaches have names like Flash of Beauty, Loblolly Bay, and Cow Wreck; all are dotted with bar-and-grills cooking up the freshest lobster in the Caribbean and serving freshly juiced mango daiquiris.

As I walked along sands edged in rich turquoise waters crowned by bubbling whitecaps, a lobsterman caught my eye as he carried his day's catch down to the surfline. He pulled in his trap from the knee-deep water and gently put his lobsters inside to keep them alive until someone ordered one (as everybody does). The tasty crustaceans then come straight out of ocean water and into the kitchen.

"Aren't you afraid someone will steal your lobsters?" I asked.

"No, mon. We don't do that kind of stuff around here," he said with the same relaxed smile that every local greeted me with.

"Everyone you pass says 'good morning' with a friendly face," a man named Sweet Tony told me. "We were brought up to be that way. Call it our nature. You see, we didn't grow up with the whole world on our shoulders. We grew up meeting our parents with a smile and our friends, too. Newcomers try to be serious, but end up smiling just like everybody else."

In my own experience, that easy smile shows up after the ignoble hold of tension and stress fades away and the mind starts soaking up the island's peace and quiet.

"Quietude is a real good medication," eighty-eight-year-old Reverend Vincent Smith told me as we sat in his comfy home in the tiny settlement. "It helps you relax, and relaxation is the main thing for the body. It protects you from illness.

"For example, there's no one against the other here, so we all feel settled. It doesn't mean that we like or love everybody, but we don't dislike anyone to the extent where we quarrel. We walk or drive in the night, anywhere we want to go, and we sleep with the house open. Nobody is going to do anything against you, so our mind is rested. We can sleep good. Sleep, you know, is the most important medicine of all.

"And fresh food counts, too. We farm here, no chemicals that are bad for our health. Everything is natural. We have a history of supplying vegetables, fish, and lobster to other islands, like Tortola and St. Thomas. You could go around and pick up as many lobsters as you wanted. Clams, too. Main thing's we've always had plenty of fresh food. It's still like that, just not as much lobster and fish as before.

"Remember," he said as I bade him goodbye, "quiet is medicine for the body and the soul. Seek it."

I heeded his advice, taking in every breath I could of the quiet nature of this isle: relishing the morning aromas of moist, buttery banana bread baking, swimming in the sea, napping amid the bay lavender, spying flamingoes, beach hopping, beachcombing, and eating lobster and fresh-caught fish every day. I'd wander around the general store just to look at the shelves of homemade lime marmalade, pineapple chutney, papaya hot sauce, and big glass jars overflowing with handmade sugar cakes (an old island recipe of fresh coconut, lots of ginger and sugar). And I mingled with the locals.

I'd sit with Sweet Tony and his wife in the shade of their venerable almond tree, sipping her homemade sea-grape wine or chatting over her island-famous prickly pear cactus liqueur. I learned about the simplicity of life on Anegada: where to find the fattest cows at slaughter time, how the ears of goats are marked to identify whom they belong to, the pride the islanders take in their school, the waitress at Flash of Beauty who designs and hand sews pretty island dresses, and the two policemen who have nothing to do. I slept, deep and long, every night—and I became rested, happy, and content, as tranquilized as those crowing roosters.

"Our island is a place where you don't have to pay for therapy," a local said. "It just happens naturally." In other words, tranquility is catching.

KEEP YOUR PEACE

Quietude is the antidote to stress-filled living. It allows us the opportunity to become conscious of the jostling effects of confusion, congestion, and consumption that swallow us up, body and soul. It enables us to confront the fact that man-made noise is shattering our spirits and dismantling our health. Quiet is a spa for the spirit.

When we allow ourselves to settle into stillness, we release the habit of living haphazardly and we become blessed with epiphanies—those sudden insights of truth, honesty, and creative thought—as if some wonderful coconut has dropped on our head and knocked some sense into us. Oprah Winfrey calls these "ah-ha moments." We realize, too, that peace and quiet bring about a harmony in relationships, a combined sense of safety and freedom, an arrest of harried activity, a liberation from anxiety and tension. It's important that we recognize the healing power of turning off the cacaphony and chaos to listen to the sound of stillness and to heed its messages.

Most of us are barraged with unnerving noise every day of our life: airplanes, trucks, mufflerless motorcycles, blaring boom boxes, brazenly loud leaf blowers, chain saws and, of course, let's not forget the irritating rings of cell phones and car alarms. Scientific research suggests that noise is a "biological stressor" contributing to stress-related conditions such as high blood pressure, coronary heart disease, ulcers, colitis, and headaches. Evidence is also growing that links noise with birth defects and low-birthweight babies. Noise, in a nutshell, is the antithesis of a healthy life—and it's getting harder and harder to escape it.

But some citizens have taken action to free their world of

aggravating sounds, like in Santa Barbara, California, where fifty unpaid volunteers gathered more than nine thousand signatures on a petition to ban the "high grinding whine" of leaf blowers (which "killed the quiet of their community"). The ban passed with 54.5 percent of the vote, uniting Santa Barbara with forty other California cities and over three hundred cities nationwide that value their peace and quiet so much that their residents worked hard to take back and ensure their treasured quiet ambiance.

Most of us have been without the sense of quiet for so long, we need to relearn just how important it is to our well-being. We need to learn to relax in the stillness for it is in inner, and outer, silence that dreams are born, that positive thoughts and intent arise, and where we are able to unite with our inner wisdom to feel that refreshing sensation of life flowing with our spirit, instead of against it. We need to remember that within peace and quiet we find personal empowerment, power to hear our own thoughts, to feel the beat of our own heart, and to let our spirit fly off to, in the words of Robert Browning, "where the quiet-colored end of evening smiles."

I find my quietude twice a day when I close the curtains on the world in the practice of Transcendental Meditation, an easy way to break the pressure-tension-distraction cycle. I flow from restless to restful, from anger to peace, from preoccupation to inspiration, from competitiveness to contentment. My meditations rekindle creativity and an amiable attitude toward life; they have opened me to unbelievable experiences and marvelous opportunities that I believe I would have otherwise missed.

Of course, there are a million other ways to slip into the rapture of quiet times. All it takes is a bit of imagination for us to find what best fits our personality and the goings-on of each day: we might move a favorite easy chair to face the fireplace, turn the lights off, and just gaze into the colorful dancing flames, take a ten-minute nap, or watch the sun slowly rise before the world gets geared up.

So, no matter where we are, we must be our own peacekeepers, borrowing time from empty activities like talking on the phone or watching television. Once we start getting a daily dose of tranquillity, we'll wonder how we ever got along without it.

★ *Gaze at the world.* Gaze into the heart of a giant oak tree, sit on the steps of your home watching the bees buzz through your yard, stare into the flame of a candle, sit quietly in your gazebo and listen to the music of nature. Simply fixate your attention on one beautiful thing, breathe it in, and enjoy the single-minded quiet.

★ *Become an anti-noise activist.* Noise is an intrusion on our privacy and can be an emotional drain. Joining like-minded people in the fight against noise will give you confidence and know-how in dealing with your right to live in a quiet neighborhood, city, and world. Check "noise pollution" on the Internet for ideas, encouragement, opportunities, and guidance.

★ *Your own private Eden.* Create your own quiet sanctuary where you can reflect, pray, and dream, whether it be a quiet corner of your home or garden, a favorite blanket spread out near the edge of a pond, or a park you can retreat to on your lunch hour. Be imaginative in finding the quiet time that best fits your surroundings and schedule.

Key West, Florida

BE TRUE TO YOU

$\mathcal{I}$n April 1982, Key Westers christened their island the "Conch Republic" when they staged a secession from the United States of America. The U.S. Border Patrol had recently set up a blockade on the Overseas Highway, the one link between Key West and mainland Florida. Traffic backed up for miles, and hours, as the patrol searched each northbound car for drug runners and illegal aliens, demanding proof of citizenship from everyone.

Outraged at being treated like noncitizens, Key Westers raised the flag of the Conch Republic and handed out Conch Republic visas, border passes, and currency. Embarrassed by the international publicity of the attempted secession, the U.S. government eventually dismantled the blockade. But every April the Conch Republic celebrates its rebirth, freedom, and victory over the Border Patrol with days of fun and festivities, in grand Key West style.

That's Key Westers for you—flagrantly independent, emphatically detached, and lusciously content in living out who they are as far away from the mainland as they can possibly get without leaving the country. They follow their spirit and nourish their identity, refusing to be influenced or dazzled by much—except, perhaps, a record-breaking fish.

The island is so free-spirited that it's truly unlike any other place on the face of the earth. With the look more of a Caribbean outpost than the southernmost city of the continental United States, this two-by-four-mile isle brims with character and characters, more fun than you can shake a stick at, and a liberating attitude that embraces and encourages all to sail off the beaten path to live out the "true you" in every sense of the word.

Like a big tropical magnet, the island has drawn me for as long as I can remember. A bit bizarre, a tad roguish, a little coquettish, and a touch obstinate, it's North America's most low-key, laid-back hideaway; it blatantly flirts with everyone who hungers to elude the "designer world" of the mainland. I simply can't get enough of it, for Key West adheres to the soul-freeing, unspoken principle of honoring the uniqueness of each and every individual.

The islanders dress, or should I say, dress down, according to their whims—not to the decrees of the fashion world—wrapping themselves in comfort and brilliant color, using batik pareos for tablecloths, riding bicycles decorated in antique jewelry and, if they drive, painting their cars, in bright murals or tiled in mosaics of mirrors and tropical motifs. You'll even find city Dumpsters adorned in intricate beaded works of art. And the islanders are masters of spontaneity, sailing off to Cuba at the drop of a hat, celebrating even the insignificant, like a good day of snorkeling or the flowering of a night blooming cactus, in a grand Keys style. They cool down hot summer days with sapodilla ice cream, refuse to be awed by the rich and famous who frequent the island, and go to great lengths to protect their coral reefs and the historical integrity of Old Town.

Old Town is a magical neighborhood, with venerable homes built in the romantic grandeur of another era by sea captains who sailed the Caribbean Sea. Most are two-storied grand old dames, trimmed in gingerbread and fronted by white picket fences. Secreted behind are gardens, virtually outdoor rooms brimming with orchids, palms, local art, and baskets overflowing in seashells, all lit nightly in the glow of tiki torches and votive candles.

Freethinkers—actresses like Tallulah Bankhead, award-winning writers from Ernest Hemingway to John Dos Passos, poets like Robert Frost, artists like John James Audubon, treasure salvagers, inventors, adventurers, and drag queens—have gathered in these gardens for decades to discuss the philosophy of Ayn Rand, great times had with Tennessee Williams in his backyard gazebo, and, of course, their bold, yet unpretentious life here in one of the U.S.'s only frost-proof cities. The locals wouldn't trade it for anything because they can just be themselves—whoever they are.

Key Westers expect each other to be free in their thinking and completely liberated in their being. It's an integral part of the life force of the island, an underlying energy which has long lured literati, artists, actors, presidents, and other world leaders. They fly in to escape the confines of mainland "shoulds," those viewpoints others impose on us, threatening our creativity and ability to embrace who we really are. If you arrive in Key West disconnected from your true spirit, don't worry, it's just a matter of time before it breaks free and you rediscover who you truly are.

EMBRACE THE "PERSON" IN YOUR PERSONALITY

The world, as a whole, seldom applauds the individuality of the common man. It seems as if there's a faceless "they," those trendsetters whose sole goal seems to be to have us all look similar, think alike, and make choices with little thought for what truly fits our own exclusive style. In other words, they have taken the "personal" out of personality by telling us what colors and fabrics to wear each season, which cars elevate us to a certain status, and what cocktails to drink if we want to be part of the "in crowd."

When we add up a harried life, chaotic days, an aim to please, and a desire to impress others the woeful total is a numbing of all our senses, including our common sense—and ultimately a disconnection from our spirit. The haste of life becomes the waste of life as we apathetically go with what we're told, with what's easy, and with what the mass market dictates for us in our society. Our own uniqueness is drowned out by the "buzz" of the pack. Our one-of-a-kind spirit spirals down into an unimaginative black hole; we forget what makes each of us, as individuals, feel good down in the depths of our soul.

When it all catches up with us, as it always does, life is shadowed by a disconcerting uneasiness and, on a deeper level, a sense of loss. We forget how much we love root beer floats, the springtime scent of fresh-mowed grass, and the dreams we once had, like setting up an easel along the Seine River and painting our own view of Paris. We live a life based on "should be's," forgetting the "could be's"—those wonderful chances at living life in a way that tickles our own individual spirit.

For a long time I lived suffocating in the convention of mainland "should be's" and my ego's feigned attempts to be part of the "in crowd." I often felt the warnings my inner soul signaled, but was moving too fast in the wrong direction to pay them any mind. But I did notice that I thrived in the capriciousness of Key West, where my smile always mirrors a relaxed happiness, my feet relish the airiness of flip-flops, and my intellect takes off in new and exciting directions as unique viewpoints are espoused by the locals.

Each time I left the island and tumbled back into the madness of the mainland pace, I became more and more discontented. The inner signals kept coming; I continued to ignore them. Then one evening when I sat enshrouded in a dark cloud of self-disappointment caused by the choices I had made that week, I read the words of inspirational writer Eileen Caddy: "It is important from time to time to slow down, to go away by yourself and simply Be."

I couldn't take off for Key West, but I did head to a nearby old, rickety fishing pier where I drank a three-dollar glass of Merlot from a plastic cup and watched an incredibly large pink-orange sun melt into the Gulf of Mexico. At the final moment, before it sank completely into the sea, I realized I didn't need, or want, such a big house with rooms I seldom entered, a boring sedan that made my soul feel old, and a closetful of clothes that didn't even come close to expressing my personality. I had sacrificed deliriously delicious experiences, that made my heart hum, for experiences that yielded nothing but a bloated ego and bedeviling feelings of restlessness, dissatisfaction, and loss.

My husband and I etched out a plan of change, eventually moving to a cottage near the water and replacing the sedan with a convertible. Now my closet brims with clothes in colors and styles uniquely me.

I return to that old fishing pier quite often, to watch stingrays and manatees glide under the docks and to toast the sunset with cheap wine. It reminds me to stay true to myself, to embrace whatever makes me happy and to avoid what drags me down. And even though we're not residing in the Conch Republic, I'm living with a Key West frame of mind, where one of the most important things is simply to hold on to who I really am.

★ *Create your own style.* Shop at vintage clothing stores to find fashions with flair; find a seamstress and present her with wonderful fabric in prints you love and "uniquely you" patterns; deck yourself out in big earrings, capes, or bangle bracelets; wear a hairstyle that's right for your own personality and individually shaped face. Let your appearance paint a portrait of who you are inside.

★ *Say "adios" to compromising attitudes.* Bid adieu to flaunting: outshining the neighbors, out-dressing the girls at work, and outstripping the relatives by driving the most expensive car in the family. Instead, let your choices swell from the best you have dwelling within; form, and adopt, your own opinions rather than those of others; and live authentically, with focus on your own life and the true happiness of your own loved ones.

★ *Believe in the true you:* A "courage call" may be in order in your quest for self-actualization, so unleash your nerve, feel the empowerment, and stand steadfast in the progress of your journey, for, at times, it can get a little scary. There will be those in your life who may try to waylay your personal growth because they feel uncomfortable or threatened by the changes they see in you. But be dauntless; be resolute and believe in the "true you." Soon you'll have a schoolgirl crush on life again, enjoying those things that make your soul soar like an eagle.

Crete, the Greek Isles

DEVELOP A HEALTH CONSCIENCE

The gods of ancient Greece have been good to Crete, maybe because it's the sacred birthplace of Zeus, their supreme deity. Legend tells us he was born in one of the thousands of caves in the White Mountains (the looming "backbone" that trails down the isle like a fertile, life-giving force), nursed by Amaltheia, the honored goat, and further nourished on the velvety, golden honey of the bee-nymph, Melissa.

Within the mountains' productive valleys, and in the coastal areas, field after field is alive with the vibrant palette of fresh produce, including groves of citrus trees whose fruits are held in such high esteem that Gaea, the goddess of earth, gave them as a wedding present to Zeus and his bride, Hera. Then there are the olive trees of the goddess Athena, cultivated here for six thousand years, which many learned men through the ages have deemed the most valuable gift of the gods to mortals. Hippocrates, the Greek father of medicine, even referred to olive oil as the "greatest therapeutic" of the world.

And the beloved Dionysus, who gave the island the gift of vineyards, seems to have passed on his own vivacious personality as the essence of the very special, and very ancient, island spirit of Crete: a rousing love of life, of friendships and pleasure, of merrymaking with a dash of mischief tossed in, of its own lively music and dance—and, of course, the enjoyment of local wine sipped, always, with great food, great company, and great respect.

The food of the ancient gods became the food of the Minoans, the ancient Cretans who, five thousand years ago, in the Bronze Age were so advanced in their intellect, their love of beauty, and their talents in art, pottery, architecture, and engineering, that they are often deemed Europe's first great civilization. While excavating the famous Palace of Knossos, near the modern-day capital of Heraklion, archeologists unearthed a huge cache of *pithoi*, enormous clay vessels where the basic ingredients of their cuisine—red wine, olive oil, grains, legumes, and glistening honey—were stored.

The same foods that sustained the lives of the Minoans continue to nourish modern-day Cretans. Goats, along with sheep, still graze on the wild, aromatic herbs and grasses that carpet the mountain slopes, their milk turned into rounds of soft cheeses. Beehives are an indispensable element of the flowering countryside, vegetables and fruits grow in profusion, and citrus and olive groves and vineyards continue to blanket the island. It's an unbroken legacy of health.

This landscape of life's nurturing ingredients is the basis for a scrumptious culinary style deemed by the world's scientific community as the healthiest on the planet, blessing the islanders with the lowest heart disease and cancer mortality indices in the world. The results of the Cretan diet are a happy, healthy longevity, a penchant for celebrating mealtimes, and a spirited affection for living.

Nowhere is this love of life more apparent than in the ancient city of Chania, where romance swirls around its old Venetian harbor like some poetic, magical spell cast by a benevolent god. The old-world architecture, painted in Mediterranean colors like pale corals, is accented by dense walls of magenta bougainvillea and windows dressed in bright and airy handmade lace. This postcard setting is perched on the harbor, protected from the Sea of Crete by an antiquated breakwater crowned by a lighthouse sporting a romantic, venerable Venetian charm dating back to the fourteenth century.

To me, Chania is lit with a touch of the exotic. Its subtle aroma is a sensual mix of the saltiness of sea air, eucalyptus trees, and just a hint of tanning hides. Mustached men peddle handcrafted Turkish knives engraved with poetry (a leftover from Turkish occupation), and vendors' carts brim with the snacks of Crete, all kinds of dried fruits and nuts. Fishermen head in from the sea, captaining bold-colored boats filled with their catches, and once ashore, with chores finished for the day, head to *tavernas* for *ouzo* (the anise-flavored Greek liqueur), hearty laughter, and traditional dancing.

As evening gives way to darkness, the beacon of the lighthouse marries the silvery glow of old-world streetlights casting a romantic glow over the Old Quarter. My husband and I deemed it the ideal moment to climb aboard a horsedrawn carriage for a slow ride through the narrow old alleyways. It was the perfect way to bide time until 10 or 11 P.M., the customary dinner hour which serves as a daily mini-celebration enjoyed with friends, discussing life, solving problems, and partaking in meals so delicious that no one ever stops to think about their benefits for the body and soul.

Every night we'd seek out a different waterfront café in which to dine and gaze upon the late-night magical aura of the harbor. Dinner was always a leisurely, delectable feast starting with appetizers like *tsatsiki* (a cucumber dip for dunking raw veggies) and *dolmades* (stuffed grape leaves in olive oil) and crispy Greek salads piled high with olives, cucumbers, tomatoes, beets, and feta cheese. Entrees of whole baked fish or the island's signature seafood mixed grills were served on huge platters, surrounded by vegetables galore, and baskets held dark, chewy bread moistened by dipping torn-off chunks into glistening, golden olive oil. The waiters kept pitchers filled with local barrel wine that flowed throughout the whole meal, accompanied by the song of good times ringing out in the night air. It's the Cretan table at its best—a most delicious way to serve up a life of health and happiness to everyone!

NOURISHING WAYS

We now have scientific proof of the very powerful link between our state of health and what we eat, especially when the ingredients are raised with respect for the land and the people it's feeding, an essential of good old-fashioned nutrition. But ancient cultures, like the Minoans and others, never doubted the fact that pure, natural foods hold the key to good health. In fact, the Chinese scholar Lin Yü-t'ang tells us, "The Chinese do not draw any distinction between food and medicine."

The thought of healthy eating, however, seems to ruffle many of our feathers. We've made a distinction between foods by calling those with life-sustaining capabilities "health food" which, in itself, suggests that other victuals are "unhealthy"; we've nicknamed those who opt for fresh, vitamin-brimming cuisine as "health nuts" simply because they put thought and intent into choosing what goes into their bodies.

The islanders of Crete have never equated their enviable

cuisine to eating "health food" or refered to themselves as "health nuts" because they enjoy every tasty morsel and reap the benefits of a culinary ethic that has never broken away from the nutritional legacy of their forebears. They simply eat the traditional fresh foods birthed by their rich, fertile soil, sweetening dishes with golden raw honey straight from the hive or grape juice fresh-pressed from the grapes (as opposed to empty refined sugar), enhancing flavors with fresh herbs and spices, and rarely eating red meat.

Cretans eat four times more fruit than southern Europeans, six times more than northern Europeans, and consume three times more vegetables than Europeans in general, putting them at the top of the list of healthy eating. This is thought to be the defining difference between Cretan-style dining and other Mediterranean diets. Olive oil, believed to be the most health-giving ingredient on Crete's menu, is utilized in every conceivable way, from drizzling and dipping to tossing and sautéing. The payoff is not a "diet" at all, but a luscious cuisine that outpowers disease, lethargy, headaches, stomach problems, and emotional vulnerability.

Herbert Spencer once wrote: "The preservation of health is a duty. Few seem conscious that there is such a thing as physical morality." It's time we forge ahead with a newfound "health conscience" of our own, making educated selections between health-giving food and health-taking food. It's time to slow down and consciously curb our desires for quick, fatty, milky, sugary foods injected with growth hormones, antibiotics, toxins, and things we can't pronounce and haven't a clue as to what they are. Instead, treat your health to a Cretan-style table, filled with those foods whose contents are pure and fresh. Sit down and comfortably enjoy mealtimes with an aura of leisure and love and tread the culinary road of the ancient and modern people of Crete by benefiting from the foods of the gods.

☆ *Think "farm fresh."* Farmers markets offer action-packed palettes of fresh herbs, organic veggies, high-quality fruit, just-laid eggs from free-roaming chickens, edible flowers, morning-baked breads, raw honey, and flavor-infused olive oils that can inspire even the most dedicated of junk food junkies to eat healthier. Food shopping takes on the outdoor pleasures of fresh air and morning sunshine mixed with the chance to meet and greet those who grow the food and others who have a healthy take on eating. A visit to these markets is also a great "field trip" for children to learn the joy—and art—of picking out the freshest ingredients and how to make healthier food choices.

☆ *Join the honey bunch.* It's no secret that refined sugar isn't the best thing in the world for us, or our kids. Sweeten up your kitchen the healthy way by checking out honey cookbooks that easily substitute this nutritious and delicious nectar of the gods for empty white sugar in everything from spaghetti sauce to pumpkin pie.

✴ *Decode the jargon.* Food manufacturers know you're in the dark when it comes to the meaning of those alien-sounding ingredients that seem impossible to pronounce, and most of us are unaware of their effects on the body and mind. Define, research, and discover what they are, as well as their possible consequences to your, and your family's, health, and then choose wisely. If you don't do this for yourself, no one else will.

✴ *Give yourself an oil upgrade.* Oil up! Replace butter and all other oils with a good extra-virgin olive oil and enjoy not only great taste, but also a healthy habit.

Oahu, Hawaii

✴

SEIZE THE MOMENT

In Hawaii, I'm a *ha'ole*, a non-Hawaiian, a Caucasian, but one totally enamored with all that is Hawaiian: chanting in a powerful ancient language; dancing with swaying hips and graceful hands that tell fascinating stories without words; healing in the natural, old-island ways with the restorative massage strokes of *lomi lomi* and with medicinal plants gathered in traditional methods; stringing *leis* from island orchids; and—surfing.

Surfing was the sport of ancient Hawaiian chiefs and kings. It has been said that, unlike other island cultures, they viewed the mighty, powerful waves not with fear of the havoc they could wreak on the island communities, but as a source of pure, unadulterated fun. Their favorite playground was a serene little village named *Waikiki* for the "spouting waters" that filled their days with challenging, free-spirited pleasure.

Waikiki Beach is highly charged with the heat of "surfing fever," an energy that ignites a carpe diem take on life and a resolution to enjoy each moment, and each wave, to its fullest. This glorious, infectious attitude is easily caught: just take a stroll along the beach sizzling with boogie boarders, outrigger canoe paddlers, and surfers galore either carrying their boards down to the water, paddling out to the surfline, or getting "stoked"—and feel that adrenaline high of riding a wave.

It all starts each morning when the "dawn patrol" paddles out to the surfline, sitting patiently in the stillness of the early phase of daybreak as the sun begins to rise over the craggy summit of Diamond Head, poised to catch the first good wave of the day. They come to get energized and to relax—to start off the morning on a high note—before changing and heading on into the office. Chances are they'll be back when the five o'clock trumpet shell blows.

These are the surfers, the *he'e nalu*, who balance their passion for surfing with the professions that physically take them away from the sea; but the lure of the waves never really leaves their thoughts. They tune in to the surfing report every chance they get, feel the beckoning of the ocean throughout the day, and, sometimes, when the roar of the waves simply refuses to be ignored, they'll duck out of the office and seize the day, surfer-style.

The other type of *he'e nalu* are the famous beachboys of Waikiki. Surfing is like a religion to them, a lifestyle where they live, eat, and breathe the sport. They make an honest living at the surf shacks teaching tourists, renting boards, and captaining outrigger canoe rides, which give visitors just a tiny taste of what catching a wave is all about. On their days off, they go surfing. And if the surf's up on the North Shore, the home of those powerful walls of water that can reach thirty-five feet, they're honor bound to seize the moment and follow their passion—whenever it presents itself and wherever it takes them.

Beachboys are mellow, laid-back, suntanned, and extremely fit mostly-older guys who've been surfing for twenty to fifty years. They have an enviable flair for looking half their age, and have made a conscious decision to spend their days outdoors with the spirit of the sea, feeling its power, its joy, its own special rush. It's a lifestyle that totally agrees with them.

Both types of *he'e nalu* have a lot in common: they deem surfing the supreme natural high; they're addicted to the individual freedom found within the sport and, like most who live out the *aloha* spirit, they measure their wealth in experiences and relationships rather than in dollars and cents. They all also worship Duke Paoa Kahanamoku, a descendent of Polynesian royalty, surfer extraordinaire, gold medal Olympic swimmer, and the "International Father of Modern Surfing," a title he earned by introducing the sport to Australia, New Zealand, and the Atlantic coast of the United States in the early 1900s.

The beachboy territory of Waikiki serves as backdrop for a gleaming seventeen-foot bronze statue of Duke. Standing royally tall in front of his surfboard, passers-by reverently lay fresh *leis* in his outstretched hands and at his bare feet. In the waters beyond, in 1929, Duke rode "a monster wave for 1⅛ miles, probably the longest ride in modern times"; and just a few blocks away, on the ground floor of the Outrigger Waikiki On The Beach hotel, vintage photos and surfing memorabilia of the Hawaiian hero cover the walls of Duke's Canoe Club, the most happening beach bar on the island.

On the golden sands hosting surfboards galore, I asked Tommy Faainuinu for a surfing lesson. This sixty-year-old Samoan, who attributes his thirty-sevenish youthful looks to his last twenty years as a beachboy, put me through the basics on the beach, towed me out to the surfline, and pointed my board shoreward. Before the lesson was half over, I was up and surfing, adrenaline pumping, feeling more alive than I had in years, embracing one of the sport's spiritual highs: it's simply impossible to feel unhappy when you're surfing!

Tommy followed my last roaring wave ride in and calmly said, "We'd better quit now. It's really not a good day for a beginner, the waves are too high and getting higher by the minute."

"Why didn't you tell me that before my lesson?" I asked.

"Then you wouldn't have gone out," he said. "You would've passed up the opportunity and maybe you wouldn't have come back. Seize the moment! That's how we think."

WHEN OPPORTUNITY KNOCKS, OPEN THE DOOR

"Surfers are very passionate in their pursuit of the best waves," Surfing Hall of Fame inductee and local senator Fred Hemmings told me. "And because of the very nature of surfing, they're also very tuned in to seizing the moment, that carpe diem attitude. With surfing you have to be in the right place at the right time, or moment, as the case may be, to surf the best wave."

But this is more than just a surfing mantra, it's a recipe for living life to its fullest. Adopting this state of mind allows you to make the most of what each day offers, engage in what speaks to your soul, cherish your blessings, and enjoy a healthy balance between the purposes of work and play, between rest and activity. It's about keeping your eyes, and your mind, open and maintaining enough flexibility to take advantage of opportunities when they come knocking.

Cultivating a talent for seizing the day, versus letting the day seize us, is one of the most exhilarating things we can do for ourselves. We learn to extend invitations to the universe to grace us with all kinds of amazing possibilities, keep ourselves bonded with the power of the positive, reify chances to follow our passions, and delve into new adventures, thus elevating our day-to-day experiences to grand new levels.

When opportunity knocks it's important to welcome it with a loving *aloha* spirit and be willing and open to grab what is being offered at the moment it presents itself, for opportunity can be very fleeting and fickle. If we hesitate, ignore, or neglect its gifts, opportunities for soul-thrilling moments abandon us in a flash. It's as if the spirit is off in the blink of an eye, seeking someone who recognizes its potential and embraces it with wide open arms—and runs with it. In the meantime, we've turned our back, once again, on what may be our own life's equivalent to the perfect wave.

When we lose our knack for seizing the day, we get lazy, too comfortable with the familiar and routine. Procrastination reigns, excuses of all kinds become habitual, weariness clouds our judgment, and our days are deprived of those spiritual adventures that make life worth living. Then somewhere down the road we're filled with regret for lost opportunities and, thus, a loss of life-inspiring events. We think of the Caribbean cruise we let slip through our fingers, the tango lessons we turned our back on, the chance to sing professionally we were afraid to take, or even little things, like missed occasions to see a play, share homemade ice cream with a best friend, or mail a birthday card.

Seizing the moment, surfer-style, doesn't necessarily require a carefree spirit, just more of a free spirit—free of the fear that keeps us from trying things we dream of; free from the rushed pace of events that keep us from seeing opportunities, let alone seizing them; free from the fatigue that smothers the flames of our desires; and free from a tendency to think of everyone else first, neglecting our own cravings for fun, fulfillment, and excitement.

"We owe it to ourselves to grab every opportunity to unite with the sea," a Hawaiian friend said, "to be able to surf when the waves are just right. That's what life is all about: doing what you like, what keeps you feeling peaceful and balanced. This is a surfer's lesson for the whole country."

★ *The present is a gift.* Live in the present moment, not in the past or the future. Slow down, look, listen, and acquaint yourself with the gifts, the messages, and the possibilities offered by the here and now—and act on them.

★ *Stay wakeful to catch the waves.* It's pointless to tune in to the possibilities within your day if you're too weary to see straight; it's impossible to be open to potentials if all you're craving is a few hours' sleep. Fatigue imprisons our enthusiasm, our spontaneity, and our will to balance work and recreation.

★ *Adopt a surfer attitude.* Ride the waves of life with passion, make the day your own, and open your door as wide as you can when opportunity knocks, for it cannot only bring spiritual spice to your life; it can make dreams come true. Remember: timing is everything.

Hong Kong Island, China

UPHOLD TRADITIONS

*H*ong Kong Island is one of the world's most exotic ports of call, a seductress of mystery, electrically charged and inundated with dramatic contrasts that blend in perfect harmony. Venerable temples crowned in upturned roofs rest peacefully within the shadows of ultramodern architectural marvels stretching skyward; old-time sampans share the waters of Victoria Harbour with gleaming streamlined yachts from the most romantic places in the world; steamy little noodle shops neighbor elegant restaurants renowned for world-class fine dining; and reflections of "old China" are mirrored in the vitality, colors, and scents of outdoor markets spilling over the alleyways that intersect with streets touted worldwide for high finance, high tech, and high fashion.

This international city of prosperity is tempered by humility, its enterprise modulated by honor, and its quick pace becalmed by inner peace. Hong Kongers inherently seek balance in everything—between land and water, nature and man, old and young, yin and yang. Their spirits embrace ancient traditions, ceremonies, and connections with ancestors who have passed on, and their intellects find fascination with omens, legends, and symbolism that bring good fortune, as I quickly discovered.

"See those mountains over there on the Kowloon side of the harbor?" my taxi driver asked as we drove in from the airport. "Nine dragons have long dwelt in the peaks of those mountains. It is said that they bathe in the sea every morning. They're strong, good natured, and bestow upon us good fortune and wellbeing. They watch over us."

"Have you ever seen one?" I asked.

"No, they're said to be invisible to the human eye," he said sneaking a peek in his rearview mirror to catch my reaction. I noted a twinkling in his eyes—one-third serious, one-third reverent, one-third fun.

He told of another legendary dragon who spends his nights sleeping in the hillside overlooking Repulse Bay and plays by day, just beyond, in the South China Sea. Developers, building a towering high-rise with a commanding view of the water, were reluctant to tempt bad luck by blocking the dragon's route from the hill to the sea. As with most of the island's architectural wonders, the wisdom of a fung shui master was sought, a thousands-year-old tradition that brings harmony between man and nature, and thus fosters prosperity and good fortune.

His esteemed advice: a "dragon-sized circular window" placed in the center of the skyscraper so the dragon could flow through, unimpeded, on his way to the bay. The architect agreed, the dragon remains happy and playful and, I must admit, it's a beautiful sight to round the curve of the seaside road and see the rich, green slopes where the dragon resides so uniquely displayed through the center of the building. Man, nature, and legends were blended to perfection thanks to an island's union with ancient traditions. The unique atmosphere this union creates is one of Hong Kong Island's greatest appeals.

Time-honored customs, rituals, and rites have endured on the island, instilling the postive edge of intent, the excitement of anticipation, and the dazzle of celebration into everyday things. Theirs is a common thread of cultural continuity that dates back eons, a bond in thoughts, words, and deeds based on a commonality of beliefs; theirs is a reverence for the delightful ways of their forebearers that stimulate, energize, and make life more special.

Hong Kong Islanders kick off mornings under fluttering fishtail palms and flowering orchid trees and amid the sounds of flowing streams and trickling fountains where tai chi is practiced to awaken and balance energy. Lunch hours often foster spiritual contemplation with visits to temples like Mo Man (Hong Kong's oldest), where people can offer kumquats and oranges (symbols of prosperity) to the deities while kneeling before ornate altars, shaking fortune-telling *chim* sticks in bamboo cylinders, and inhaling the fragrance of the gigantic coils of incense that blanket the ceiling. Special attention is paid along the way to transforming everyday activities (like drinking a simple cup of hot tea) into venerable ceremonies, to looking back to ancient uses of traditional herbs and acupuncture for healing, and to incorporating symbols of good fortune (like peach blossom trees, even numbers, the prosperous colors of red and gold) and certain ingredients (which are either chosen or avoided) into the meals, spread on huge lazy Susans centered on dining tables, that last for hours.

Carrying out traditions is a way of living, and believing, which exemplifies David Hume's words: "Custom, then, is the great guide of human life." Many consider it to be a balancing lifestyle that has helped Hong Kong Island become an unparalleled world of prosperity and creative possibilities.

OUR RITES

Traditions, rites, and rituals slow us down and lead us home when we feel as though we have lost our way. They return us to a place of constancy, familiarity, and comfort, plant our feet more firmly on the ground, and give us a sense of belonging to a whole rather than living as an isolated part of something we don't quite connect with. They unite us with a special part of our inner being and awaken the character of ancestors whose essence flows through our veins.

Most of us have become too busy, too preoccupied, and too exhausted to even think about the importance tradition plays in our lives. But the reality is that there's nothing better for a worn-out, harried soul than to be held in the security, the certainty, and the stability of rituals, whether they spring from the spirit of our forebears, are born out of our own creative flair, or combine a little of both.

Customs infuse our experiences with meaning and significance, and give us an opportunity to make life feel extraspecial. But the energy we put into upholding tradition, or creating new ones, often declines as our own private worlds spin faster, both inside and out. For speed breeds forgetfulness, carelessness, and an inability to create memorable magical moments from the commonplace. All it takes is one broken link in a chain of generations for traditions to get lost, and, along with them, our connections to them and our past. It simply becomes too much of a chore to get out the family china for special occasions and soon it just sits, unused, in the cabinet. We deprive ourselves of the fun of reveling in ceremonious customs, like drinking green beer at the local Irish pub on St. Patrick's Day or being electrified by the fireworks bursting right over our heads at our city's Fourth of July observances, because we're too tired; we lose our customs because we try to outdo what has been done by our forebears, just to impress others. Then when it all becomes too much we lose our enthusiasm to keep tradition going. We abandon it altogether.

But the mindset of previous generations was never "bigger and better," rather it was a handing down and preserving of the simple: a hand-iced Betty Crocker devil's food cake topped in birthday candles, passing around Great Grandma's crystal gravy boat on Easter, rooting for Yale's football team because your great-great-grandfather did, a family picnic every June, or celebrating Shabbat dinner every Friday night. These are the kinds of traditions we can easily preserve without elaborate plans, the kinds that reconnect us with who we are and the world we live in, the kinds that light our inner glow. These are the customs that instill a sense of purpose, excitement, and meaningful union with our present family as well as those we keep alive in spirit by honoring a few of their impulses and knacks for making life more enjoyable.

There's no better time than the present to inspire our lives with traditions and rituals, to find balance in their grounding power, to find guidance in their wisdom. Remember that anything done with just an ounce of special thought becomes a tradition with repeated practice. Recall the words of philosopher

Friedrich Nietzsche: "Every tradition grows ever more venerable.... The reverence due to it increases from generation to generation. The tradition becomes holy and inspires awe."

✫ *Embrace new traditions.* Open yourself to the joy of the customs of others. Investigate the history and fun of piñatas, of Chinese Lunar New Year, of Greek dances—and let the good times roll!

✫ *Indulge in individual rituals.* Personal rituals are a vital part of life. They can range from a big bowl of popcorn enjoyed alone, all wrapped up in the warmth of the afghan your grandmother crocheted, to a special Saturday walk to the local botanical gardens with your dog, to a trip to a traditional vacation spot you eagerly await every year.

✫ *Investigate your family's customs.* Delve into a family research project, unearthing the customs of the countries of your ancestry and incorporating some of them into your life: music and legends, beliefs and superstitions, food and drink. Or, ask your parents what special rituals they remember from their childhood. They will add special significance to your daily practices and carry more of your ancestral ties into the future.

★ *Take an honest assessment of your observances.* Which traditions have you continued with joy and reverence? If there are none, analyze why you have chosen to break with the traditions of your family—are you too tired, discouraged by your spouse or in-laws to keep your own ancestral connection alive? Or have you fallen into the trap of doing nothing rather than carrying out your rite in a simpler fashion?

Jamaica

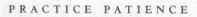

PRACTICE PATIENCE

*Y*ea, mon! It's Jamaica—sittin' ninety miles south of Cuba, this independent island nation sings songs of solidarity and strength, dances to the island-born Rastafarian rhythm of reggae, and captures the very essence of the Jamaican soul in its colorful art. The islanders boast a multicultural beauty both in physical and spiritual character: they are dignified, poised, and have a great sense of pride and an exceptional flair for patience. They possess the particular Jamaican talent for lively, lighthearted living and extracting the best of what their circumstances have to offer.

The isle itself is a package of adventure and wonder wrapped in stunning Caribbean beauty, generous in opportunities to hike the rugged Blue Mountains (which Columbus named for their unusual hue), to stroll glades and gullies of thick green ferns, to climb the rocky tiers of cool waterfalls cascading down to the sea, to canter horses through jungle-thick rain forests, and to tread in the rum-drinking footsteps of infamous pirates like Blackbeard and Calico Jack.

The first thing I do when I come to Jamaica is bury my watch in the suitcase and set my inner clock to the island's pure tropical tranquillity—that slow-cooking joy that the islanders create just by viewing time in their own unique way. Then I find a seat in a local beachside eatery, order up some jerk chicken, and listen to the locals talk "Jamaican talk," their musical patois of African languages, French, and Spanish mixed with their own fun ways with words so unique even other islands of the Caribbean have a difficult time gettin' it all.

"Doctor Breeze" is their name for the trade winds that blow in over the Caribbean Sea to cool an island day. The doctor just makes everything feel "irie," they say, i.e., simply wonderful. And if the bus, your dinner, or your guide is late, someone calmly says, "Soon come." Translation: It'll happen sooner or later, just relax.

It doesn't take long to begin to appreciate this "soon come" take on life. It's the essence of island time: being guided by patience and refusing to allow obstacles, problems, or delays to trigger high blood pressure, stress, anger, or frustration. Instead, Jamaicans are very forgiving of the moment regardless of what's happening; it's a "don't worry, be happy" kind of philosophy, a belief that all, in its own good time, will "soon come."

The choice to embrace the virtues of patience allows the locals to accept the quirks of island life: late mail, tires blowing after hitting giant-sized potholes flushed out by gulleywashers, waiting for fish to bite or the band to start playing, electrical outages, and the like. But with patience it is, as the locals say, a "cool running." Everything is easy.

The epitome of the island's famous forbearance is the Jamaican Bobsled Team. Back in the fall of 1987, some members of the Jamaican Defence Force tried out for the first tropical island team to compete in the winter Olympics, even though they were short on money, had never seen snow, and had never seen, let alone ridden in, a bobsled. They knew, however, that they would give other teams a run for their money in the all-important push start, something they were used to from the isle's famous pushcart derbies. So they stayed true to their vision and were patient, in the strictest sense of Webster's definition: "steadfast in the face of adversity." They were always looking up, not down, always keeping their sights on the positive, and, in true Jamaican spirit, always ready to enjoy the journey. This one led them to the 1988 Calgary Winter Olympic Games.

There they gave their best, in spite of setbacks, and maintained their dignity, survived a crash that left spectators from around the world holding their breath (me included!), and with that sense of Jamaican poise, somehow picked themselves up, held their heads high, and walked, with their bobsled, over the finish line—Jamaican-honor bound not to let the circumstances keep them from finishing the race. Their patience and determination rendered them winners in every sense of the Olympic spirit, and endeared them to the rest of the world in spite of finishing in last place. To this day, when the team comes smilin' and strollin' in, proudly representing their island in the Winter Olympics opening ceremony's Parade of Nations, the crowds cheer in ear-deafening applause for the tropical bobsledders who steadfastly never gave up.

From their humble beginning as underdogs, the powerful athletes have acquired a loyal worldwide following and have had many shining moments: in the 1994 Olympics they placed fourteenth, ahead of Japan, the United States, Russia, and France; in 2000 they took gold in three events at the World Push Championships in Monte Carlo, and in 2002 at the Salt Lake City Winter Olympics, the two-man team placed a respectable 28 out of 37 and set a track start Olympic record in the process. (Lack of funds sadly kept the four-man team from competing.) Not too shabby for reggae-dancing islanders who had never walked on ice and were terribly short on cash, but who overflowed in patience, persistence, and determination.

And the Olympic gold? Yea, mon, soon come!

STAND STEADFAST

To cultivate patience is just the "irie" thing for all of us to do. Patience gifts us with a different take on things: we ease up on situations and forgive the imperfections in ourselves, others, and our circumstances. It's a virtue that gives us the upper edge in life, inspiring us to stay more relaxed about things, to complete what we start (no matter what happens), to act instead of react, and to sustain focus. Patience rescues us from a pressure-cooker lifestyle because we give up living in a restless state of urgency and stop responding to every obstacle like it's a personal assault.

While many of us might think of patience as backing down or as a sign of weakness, it's actually an extremely empowering tool. It bestows us with a strong advantage over those with impatient ways, for we hold on to our demeanor, reply to the world with finesse, think instead of rant, rave, and whine. We go with the flow instead of pushing and squeezing down on life, and we realize that contending with minor difficulties is simply the way of things and thereby inject balance and more joy into our days. It also breeds persistence. Like the Jamaican Bobsled Team, patient people set their sights high on goals they're determined to accomplish and don't get distracted when nothing happens overnight. Even in the face of misfortune, patient people just seem to have a knack for landing in the right place at the right time.

Impatient living is rash, hasty living. Instead of patiently saving for a new dress, for example, we plunk it on a credit card, adding more to our debt and thus more worries to our lives. Even an impatient scowl, that unconscious show of rage and furor, can alter our lives in ways we aren't even aware of, causing relaxed, restful people to go out of their way to avoid our difficult, stressed out, complaining nature. We may forgo action and, consequently, miss our chance of shining. We take the easy way out and settle for less, maybe even settling for an unsuitable mate because we feel the insistence of immediate gratification. And often impatience goads us into abandoning our dreams because we get discouraged and panicked when the going gets tough. But, hey, mon, that's just part of living.

When we find ourselves sliding into the groove of "soon come" we benefit from a patient island-style peace, and our minds remain relaxed and open and our tempers in check. It's just like the French poet Jean La Fontaine wrote, "Patience and passage of time do more than strength and fury."

Adopting that patient "soon come" state of mind comes with rewards of all kinds. Those drowsy, slow rides on homemade bamboo rafts down Jamaica's Rio Grande River are mind-massaging reminders of the value of just floating on the currents the universe offers. The islanders' easy, liquid movements, which naturally accompany the rhythm of reggae, express their patient and accepting dance with life, which protects them from the ravages of stress. And when visitors come to the island and find themselves in wait of culinary delights like the slow-grilled, peppery, melt-in-your-mouth Jamaican jerk chicken, they learn to take advantage of the delay by relaxing into the island time so pervasive here. For everything just simply "soon comes."

---

* *Practice patience.* If you catch yourself punching the elevator button more than once, stop and ask yourself, "Why?" Come to a complete stop at a yellow light before it turns red, mosey home the long way, stopping at the beach, woodlands, or a garden for a few minutes' respite, and always count to ten before reacting.

* *Learn to wait constructively.* Bring along a book of inspirational quotes, repeat positive affirmations, write letters or poetry, or simply practice breathing and meditation instead of fuming while you wait.

* *Stop whining!* Set aside one day a week specifically as "No Complaint Day," with a mission not to whine or utter one word of complaint for twenty-four hours.

★ *Choose to defuse.* When you feel your blood pressure skyrocketing, when you feel that sense of urgency bearing down on you, when you feel as if you want to rant and rave, simply choose not to. Just think, "Soon come," smile ... and enjoy the moment.

Santa Catalina Island, California

BE A FRIEND TO MOTHER EARTH

*I*f the streets of the tiny valley village of Avalon could talk, what tales they would tell! The most glittering stars of Hollywood's golden era, as well as many presidents and heads of state, have often sought the "far away" feel of Santa Catalina Island, even though its just twenty-six miles from the southern coast of California.

As I strolled the seaside Via Casino, the pedestrian promenade shaded by a queue of Canary Island date palms, I found it easy to imagine John Wayne at the helm of his yacht putting in at Avalon Harbor; Stan Laurel (of Laurel and Hardy) weighing

in his big game fish on the Green Pleasure Pier; and island home-
owners like Marilyn Monroe, Jean Harlow, or Johnny "Tarzan"
Weissmuller strutting their stuff down Crescent Avenue to the
huge, fancy ballroom of the Art Deco Catalina Casino—famous
not for gambling, but for the dance music of the best of live big
bands, like Tommy Dorsey and Harry James.

Along the way they'd pass the masculine old elegance of the
world-renowned Avalon Tuna Club, the oldest fishing club in the
United States, perched above the clear waters of the harbor, which
flicker with the lightning-bright orange of garibaldis, California's
protected state fish. Its famous porch has long been a gathering place where fish tales are swapped by the club's "gentlemen
anglers" who read like a list of Who's Who—from Charlie Chaplin
and Bing Crosby to Teddy Roosevelt and Sir Winston Churchill—
all of whom honored the distinguished club's pioneering spirit of
good sportsmanship, angling ethics, and catch-and-release conscience now adopted by fishing clubs around the globe.

The Tuna Club was founded in 1898 by one of the island's
early pioneers, naturalist, sportsman, and *Los Angeles Times* editor Charles Holder. He had been lured to Catalina Island to challenge the big game fish that flourished in the surrounding waters,
but what he found horrified him: unconscionable fishing tech-
niques, an outrageous number of fish being caught, and the pure
waste of magnificent game fish like leaping yellowtail tuna,
broadbill swordfish, and marlin. Determined to safeguard this
precious resource, he formed the club, drew an enviable, distin-

guished membership, and established the ground-breaking conservation stance that put Catalina Island on the map.

Holder was not alone in his love for Catalina's precious natural splendor. When you stand on the docks of the Tuna Club and look across the crescent-shaped harbor, a gleaming white 1921 Georgian colonial house catches everyone's eye, the home that William Wrigley (of chewing gum fame) had built after he developed a lifelong crush on (and purchased most of) the island. His resolve: to preserve Catalina's natural beauty and, in the process, endow the future of many generations of islanders, and visitors, with an island and a lifestyle where mountains and quiet little coves remained untouched by development.

Consequently, canyon slopes are steep and beautiful, dotted in the creamy-yellow flowers of poppy trees, St. Catherine's lace, which changes from springtime white to summer beige and deep russet in the fall, and the Christmas-red fruit of prickly pear cacti. Bald eagles and red-tailed hawks soar against a clear sky, quail scurry with their babies across hiking trails, and buffalo still roam deep in the interior, descendants of the small herd Cecil B. De-Mille imported in 1929 as props for a movie based on a book authored by island resident Zane Grey. And it's all protected, 86 percent of the island, under the watchful eye of the Santa Catalina Conservancy, the guardians of Wrigley's dream.

Whereas Wrigley became a patron of the land and Holder befriended the life in the surrounding waters, they both bequeathed their environmental conscience to the Catalina islanders who continue to this day to protect the enviable little world they have inherited.

"Conservation has long been an aim of our island," an islander told me. "It's the reason life is so wonderful here. We've been able to preserve the best part of our island—and island lifestyle. We haven't sold out."

The locals are more than happy to conserve water, as their only source is rainwater collected in a mountain-high reservoir. Inventive conservation measures include saltwater used in such innocuous places as fire hydrants, and homes are double plumbed so it flushes down johns in lieu of precious drinking water. They've also voluntarily restricted the number of cars on the isle and thus limited pollution and congestion: the waiting list for a car permit is ten to twelve years. And golf carts, the most common mode of transportation in Avalon, are limited to one per family to avoid overcrowded village streets, and they're strictly prohibited on the windy interior roads.

The typical harvesting of Pacific sea kelp forests as well as fishing are off limits in places like Lover's Cove Marine Preserve, teeming with vibrant fish and spiny lobster. Sport fishing rules are strictly enforced, and permits are frugally issued to hikers and campers to preserve the integrity of the land, the shoreline, and the island's wildlife. And the developers? The Conservancy has staved them off as it keeps a constant vigilance on what's going on. Consequently, the village of Avalon is the only place on the island where property can be bought—but only on the rare occasions when locals are willing to part with their little patch of protected paradise.

EXTEND A HAND

Mother Earth has been good to us. She has given us what we need to sustain life—clean air, crystal clear streams, fertile soil, her own natural medicines, and sunshine. She has also brought joy to our souls through the myriad of spectacular beauties found throughout the planet, from snow-capped mountains to incredible walls of undersea coral; she's brought comfort to us with birdsong and secret sanctuaries within forests where we can retreat when the world troubles us; she offers us rest in sleepy dark nights accented in silvery moonbeams and relaxing, cool winds. She has, in the strictest sense of the word, been a constant friend to each and every one of us.

But we've put Mother Earth through a lot in the past hundred years, inflicting and widening wounds, and taking advantage of her resources. Maybe it's time we extend the hand of friendship back.

It's really very easy. Befriending the earth simply requires that we form a bond with our surroundings and treat them as we would any cherished companion—we honor them, we give of ourselves, and we avoid hurting each other as much as possible. All it takes is a protective Catalina Island–style state of mind, where we decide to value a high-quality environment, where we acknowledge that the aesthetics of our daily surroundings can have a profound impact on how we live and feel, where the little sacrifices we make for the sake of the environment are deemed worth the results, and where growth is simply not a priority.

When we adopt a conservation stance, we become more of a protective participant in our ambiance; we go through our days with eyes wide open and vision heightened, truly seeing and watching over the scenery around us. We can guard things like giant old oaks, a habitat for cardinals, and clean shorelines and safe waters so they don't vanish and take their uplifting effects with them.

Caring about the environment is considered an innate moral obligation on so many of the world's islands because the islanders are more in tune with the dependency we all have on Mother Earth; conservation to them is just as normal as breathing. But because continents are so vast, and things so easy to come by, too many mainlanders have been a bit slow in developing an environmental conscience. Yet we've always known in our hearts that nothing is limitless, nothing inexhaustible; we know it's time to turn our attention to the sustainability of our resources and the earth's natural wonder, for once ancient trees, trout-filled streams, and apple orchards are erased from our presence, they do indeed become a thing of the past—and we, as individuals, are all the poorer for it.

✮ *Watch your water ways*. Never waste water down the drain; collect it and use it for other things, like watering a plant. Repair the drippy faucet, replace the old shower head with an ultralow flow version, and run the dishwasher only when full. For tips, visit www.waterinfo.org.

✮ *Care for the air*. Drive only when you have to. Hop on your bike, carpool, combine errands, shop via phone, mail, or the net. Investigate the possibility of buying an electric car, use solar energy.

✮ *Use moral sense*. When you hear about projects in the works that will destroy, for example, a blue jay habitat, or will foul the air or our food, deplete resources, or sully pristine environments, adopt the role of guardian. Don't patronize restaurants that feature endangered or threatened fish on their menus. Let your voice be heard, and let your environmental conscience guide your vote on election day.

✮ *Live by an environmental mantra*. "Waste not, want not; recycle and reuse."

Likiep Atoll,
the Marshall Islands,
Micronesia

LIVE SIMPLY

ake your very best fantasy about a pristine Pacific island, multiply it by about a thousand, and maybe, just maybe, you might come close to envisioning Likiep Atoll, an isolated ring of islands framing a thirty-mile-wide lagoon of gin-clear waters, lushly decorated by sky-touching coconut palms, breadfruit trees, and brilliant snow-white beach sands.

The atoll has a fascinating colonial history. During the late 1800s, when coconut oil was in great demand, businessmen Jose deBrum and Adolph Capelle bought the little bouquet of islands from Joortoka, the local chief at the time. To this day, it is the only privately owned atoll in the Marshall Islands of Micronesia. DeBrum and Capelle established an enormous coconut plantation, married Marshallese women, and lived happily, island style, until the end of their days. Their descendents still live here, around five hundred of them, mostly on the main island, Likiep, in the village the two Europeans laid out more than a hundred years ago. The original footpaths lined in old coral rock still cross the pretty little community shaded by aged big-leafed trees flowering in all colors and infusing the air with tropical perfumes. And even though the islanders work hard—the men raise giant clams for export and fish for their meals, the muumuu-clad women weave thin strips of pandanus leaves into fans renowned throughout the Pacific and prepare meals of breadfruit, coconut, and seafood outside on cook stations fired by coconut husks— the simplicity and practicality of their lifestyle allows them to live stress-free, *kelarikrik* (Marshallese for "taking in the breeze"), letting the day pass by on the *bymbe*, a "whenever," no-rush kind of pace.

One morning I sat in the shade of a shaving-brush tree in full bloom, watching Joe deBrum, mayor and patriarch of Likiep, cast a net for bait fish, tiny silver sardines he would use later to catch our dinner. "We live simply here," he told me. "It's a good life. We don't need much to be happy. That's the key."

Life is supersimple on Likiep. Homes are modest, so clean you can eat off the floor, with no furniture save for *jaki*, hand-woven mats for sleeping. The islanders get along just fine with-

out electricity, telephones, high-tech (and even low-tech) machines, stores, and most things we consider essential to life back
home. Communication with the outside world is via ham radios,
the plane arrives from Majuro twice a week bringing in relatives
and supplies like boat fuel and a little "Western food" like flour
and sugar. It's just real life—real simple.

Everyone lives by the "old folks laws," the simple, common-
sense principles that businessmen deBrum and Capelle originally
laid down. The code of conduct has rendered a very distinct culture rooted in a steadfast morality, dignity, and care-and-share attitude that serves them well. It's illegal to sell alcohol, chicken
legs are painted different colors to certify ownership, and if a pig
is slaughtered, it's shared with everyone. Every evening the curfew sounds at 8 P.M., time for all kids to be home, and again at 10
P.M., time for all adults to be home—unless they're out fishing,
which is allowed only between the hours of 6 P.M. and 6 A.M., with
rods, no hand lines. Anglers are required to leave the big fish to
reproduce and sustain the fishery that has always been there to
feed them. Naturally, they only catch what their families will
consume at mealtime, which is right-out-of-the-water-fresh and is
often eaten as *sashimi*.

This logical and uncomplicated approach to life has a wonderful influence on the island's children, who are exceptionally
gentle and well behaved, learning what's acceptable—and what's
not—early on. They're given the responsibility of helping the
family with chores, like keeping the yards clean of fallen flowers

and leaves, and tending to the chickens that roam free, all done before and after school each day. During my time on the atoll, I never heard a raised voice; there was no throwing of tantrums, no arguing, crying, or parents reprimanding their children.

Instead, boys and girls of all ages play on the beach, hugging or holding hands, all with carefree giggles. They approached me, unafraid yet with an endearing shyness, eager to try out the English phrases they learn in school, like "See you later alligator." They'd run down the beach, returning a few minutes later bearing gifts of cowrie shells; then they'd slip their warm little hands in mine and we'd stroll the waterline together.

"Remember," Joe said, "They've never seen TV so they don't know what violence, vulgar language, or hate is. We don't have those things here. It makes a difference in a child's disposition."

What the children do have are hearts that can never bestow enough on one another, and an unsurpassed gentility of spirit. The church-quiet island is enveloped by the islanders' sense of heavenly contentment with life, with who they are, and with a confidence that whatever fate may throw their way, in Likiep Atoll there is a simple solution.

PURE AND SIMPLE

To simplify our life is an act of self-love, a liberating decision that sets us up for a lighter take on life, rescues us from a fast-forward

pace, and rids us of complications, confusion, and excess—the lit-
ter of life that trips us up on a daily basis. The islanders of Likiep
Atoll know the value of keeping things sensible, sane, and simple,
for simplicity goes hand-in-hand with a frustration-free life. According to Webster the word "simple" is synonymous with pure,
perfect, easy, and royal—everyone's ideal way of being.

Even if we can't give up our beds for *jaki* or rewrite our city's
laws, we can seek that simpler road, ridding ourselves of the
deadweight of attitudes, tendencies, people, possessions, and beliefs that anchor us in stress and wasted energy. We can all reduce the complexities of daily living to the most simplistic of
elements, dealing with things more efficiently with Likiep-style
logic, freeing up our time, and avoiding chaos and aggravation.

Not long ago I ran into an acquaintance who told me how
she was following her own unique version of the American dream
by simplifying her lifestyle. Her goals: more time for herself,
more fun, more love, more meaning; less money, less status symbols, less stuff to contend with, less debt. So she downsized, ridding herself of the heavy burden of a huge home, sold her stuff
at a yard sale, decreased her work hours for her health, her family, and her sanity. The move led her downtown so she could
drive less, spend more time within the beauty of the parks now
in walking distance from her new place, and take advantage of
things like the library, city tennis courts, and jogging tracks.

This is just one person in an ever-growing number of people
who have concluded that their life is out of control. They've ap-

praised the way they spend their days, what they spend their hard-earned paycheck on, how well they know their children, and what the stress of chasing that raise or bigger home is doing to their health. These are the simplicity seekers of the twenty-first century; these are the people forming the growing resistance to the complexities of life. We invite you to join.

To initiate simplicity into our lives, we begin by modifying those things we know that we ourselves are capable of improving. It's simply a process of elimination, of discarding all unneeded steps and unnecessary items in our day—like tossing out all of those extra pillows dressed in shams, which can turn something as basic as making a bed into a complex task. We can set down simple, straightforward home rules to keep life more reasonable and rational, or ask ourselves questions that lead to better choices—like whether we really need those high-maintenance recreational toys we barely use. It's simply a matter of pinpointing what creates feelings of stress, anxiety, and defeat, and then either reducing these processes to the most basic steps, or clearing away whatever gnaws at us.

✴ *Exercise your right to simplistic encounters.* There are always simpler ways of doing things, so save your day, your health, and your time by patronizing only those businesses, from banks and repairmen to doctors and insurance companies, that make it easy

and efficient to get appointments or problems re-
solved.

⭐ *Don't overschedule.* Simplifying our schedules, including our children's, is one of the most liberating
and relaxing things we can do. Erase or condense errands. Do what you can by mail, like paying bills
and buying stamps. Take advantage of delivery or
courier services. Make lists so that you can grocery
shop efficiently, and don't commit to too many outside activities for any family member. Never plan
more than you can easily do.

⭐ *Ditch the digital.* Don't be awestruck by complex
technology that's supposed to ease our lives but
really only serves to create more headaches. Buying
cars, appliances, and electronics with simplicity and,
thus, serenity in mind will prompt manufacturers to
consider the stress levels of average consumers, and
maybe they'll try to dazzle us with simplicity, instead of complicated high tech.

St. Honorat, France

BREATHE WELL

reathe deeply," a woman said in a classy French accent as we disembarked the ferry from Cannes to St. Honorat, one of the *Îles de Lérins* of France. "It's all in the air."

"What's in the air?" I asked.

"The serenity . . . the calmness." she said. "Breathe deeply and you'll feel a change come over you, from the inside out. It's like magic."

I followed the woman along with other mainland escapees through the woodsy fragrances of towering trees, a white-flowering coastal heather, and other plants of the Mediterranean. All of us softened our voices as requested by the old wooden boards along the way, hand painted in the now-faded words: "*Silence. Merci beaucoup.*"

Soon the daytrippers started scattering, some drawn to climb out on the flat tops of massive boulders strung along the coastline, spreading beach towels and stretching out to catch rays atop sun-warmed rocks. Others placed picnic baskets (filled *à la française* with bottles of Bordeaux, *fromage* [cheese], crumbly-crusted *baguettes*, and fresh fruit) within easy reach of blankets spread upon the ground and dotted by the lacy shadows of pines so tall they seemed to brush the sky.

The natural fragrances infused the air and seemed to cast a restful, and respectful, spell over everyone. People did, indeed, start to breathe slower, deeper, and easier; facial muscles relaxed, demeanors eased, and attitudes became, well, islandy. The transformation was an unconscious one, a gradual sedation by nature's own pure aromatics: the scent of eucalyptus trees, so cooling to the body, freeing respiration and easing everyday aches and pains; the woody essence of cypress trees, aiding in relieving stress and nurturing sound, healing sleep; the uplifting smell of coastal pines, energizing and liberating us from the grips of fatigue and muscle tension. Add to this aromatherapy the bobbing colors of the Mediterranean Sea, the steady cradlesong of waves breaking against the ruggedly rocky coast, and the freshness of sea-scented air, and stress and tension just didn't stand a chance of holding on to any of us.

The essence of the island lulled me into one of those wondrous outdoor naps, where the fresh air enwrapped me like a natural, weightless comforter and the sound of a light wind stirring the trees played on as a hypnotic chant. I awoke with a smile, a deep, freeing breath, and a yearning to drift aimlessly around the isle, where I came upon one of the most beautiful sights I'd ever seen: fields of lavender in full bloom, slightly ruffled by the breeze and divinely backlit by a sky colored French-country blue and the venerable fifteen-hundred-year-old St. Honorat abbey, one of the oldest in France.

Story has it that the hermit Honoratus arrived on the isle in A.D. 410 to escape his followers but, having a change of heart, he opened a monastery instead. At one point the abbey swelled to 3,700 monks. It also turned out the likes of Ireland's famous bishop, St. Patrick. In its heyday, it was one of the most powerful religious centers in all of southern Europe, boasting ownership of the mainland coastline, which included such cities as now super-chic Cannes. But through the ages the abbey was pilfered and plundered, not only by Barbary, Genoese, and Spanish pirates, but also by "papal corruption."

Today only around forty Cistercian monks reside in the abbey, which pairs the medieval feel of its older structures with more modern nineteenth-century buildings (some of which are open to visitors). The monks carry on the age-old use of natural aromatics, keeping busy by cultivating vineyards; tending fields of lavender (an herb popularly known for calming the central nervous system, relaxing tension-riddled bodies, minds, and emotions); caring for groves of orange trees (whose perfumed blossoms, also known as neroli, are renowned in the aromatherapy world for their tranquilizing effect on the emotions of the heart as well as anxiety, grief, and excessive stress); and keeping bees to produce raw honey (whose scent offers warmth and reassurance). They are known up and down the French Riviera for "Lerina," a special liqueur they make from an ancient monastic recipe that blends about forty different aromatic plants.

The monks miraculously sustain the island's soothing environment by keeping the air brimming with the restorative aromas of the climate's native flora and maintaining silence and an aura of composure. These soothing spalike components—*au naturel*—are the reasons the French mainlanders, worldwide visitors, and yachties cruising the Mediterranean are seduced by St. Honorat. We come to calm our minds, relax our nerves, find balance, and restore our *esprit* for living life to its fullest. And we're always sure to take a piece of the island's relaxing grace home with us for future use, especially the monks' calming lavender products and, naturally, a bottle or two of Lerina.

A BREATH OF INSPIRATION

Aromas possess great powers. From the earliest of time our sense of smell has been an important and integral part of living well. It warns us of danger, lures us to food, relaxes us, triggers wonderful memories, induces appetite and sexual arousal, balances us emotionally, and assists healing on a physical, emotional, and spiritual level.

Opportunities to reinforce our health, boost mood, and inspire balanced living by inhaling aromas are endless, easy, and virtually everywhere: in trees, flowers, hay and grass, aromatic wood, storms and balmy breezes, home cooking, the natural subtle scents of one another, the bouquet of a good wine, the smell of sunshine, fresh air, and the sea, a just-bathed puppy, and crispy-clean sheets. Sometimes all we have to do is pause a bit, breathe a little deeper, and take note of what the universe readily provides; other times we can simply create aromatic atmospheres by practicing aromatherapy, keeping the flames of scented candles aglow, burning a little incense, perfuming the kitchen in cinnamon and cloves, or growing pots of fresh herbs on the porch where the stirring smells of mint, rosemary, or basil can infuse our air.

Because our sense of smell is processed in the same area of the brain as memory and emotion, aromas can trigger particular feeling and/or remembrances of precious times, special people, and extraordinary places. The smell of rum and coconut arouses visions of the Caribbean, fresh-brewed coffee and bacon and eggs warm us with thoughts of family breakfasts on snowy mornings, and scents of summer showers allow us to relive romantic strolls. For me, lavender always brings to mind the fields of St. Honorat.

Such positive emotions and stirring memories nourish us with lighter, happier attitudes and, thus, keep us in a more contented state, better able to fend off stress, tension, and worry.

Given our modern tendency to be preoccupied and rushed, we all too often ignore the scents that float our way; when we live where air is fouled or where nature is replaced by man-made materials, our sense of smell becomes clouded, assaulted, or falls prey to deprivation. Unfortunately, we simply don't tune in to the aromas of life like we used to, resulting in what archeologist and aromatic consultant John Steele describes as olfactory "sensory amnesia," a decreased awareness of smell. We're letting the delights of fragrance pass us by.

Fortunately, we can take our cue from St. Honorat and learn to create harmony, healing, and health in our lives through the use of aromatics and the art of aromatherapy, one of the wisest and easiest practices of self-care. Aromatherapy makes use of botanicals, which cultures have cherished for thousands of years: the Egyptians were masters of botanicals, the Greeks used them to give their athletes an edge, the Romans became so impressed with their healing prowess that they imported more than three thousand tons of frankincense (which has analgesic and anti-inflammatory properties) and around six hundred tons of myrrh (an expectorant, antiseptic, and antispasmodic) from the Arabs.

The essential oils, the "life force," of the botanicals used in aromatherapy (and available in small vials from many New Age or natural foods stores) can restore imbalances, facilitate mental clarity, gift us with energy, enthusiasm, and high self-esteem, keep us from slipping into worry, anxiety, and fear. They can come to our rescue in times of stomach aches and urinary problems, can aid in reducing blood pressure, ease PMS and menopause symptoms, or even fight depression and reduce pain. But more important, they offer us a simple way to infuse our lives with the earth's heavenly, healing aromas and create a virtual garden when we can't have the real thing.

★ *Unwind with lavender.* Capture the fields of St. Honorat by misting lavender on your pillow before going to bed, swirl it into a hot tub, try a foot soak in lavender-infused warm water for twenty minutes, place a lavender sachet in your lingerie drawer, or place a potted lavender plant where you can pinch off a bit, stash it in an easy-reach pocket, and sniff it the moment stress hits.

★ *Traffic tamers.* Defuse road rage with a car aromatherapy diffuser (not to be confused with those sick-smelling cardboard deodorizers that hang from mirrors in taxicabs). Just pour an essential oil into a pretty little amphora made from clay (a natural diffuser), hang it from the rearview mirror, and breathe in the subtle scent; or fill a diffuser that plugs into a cigarette lighter to warm up and disperse the fragrance. Vanilla softens anger and frustration, cinnamon supports the heart, lavender and orange blossoms calm, lemon, lime, and eucalyptus energize, peppermint aids breathing.

★ *Fill the world with fragrance.* Environmental aromatherapy is catching on in cities around the globe. Lead your community to plant and save trees and plants with aromatic qualities to ensure that the design of public spaces includes a beautiful variety of fragrances; follow the lead of some European and Asian cities that infuse crowded places like subways with lavender to soothe away tension and frustration.

★ *Aromatize your atmosphere.* Dress your yard in fragrant flowers and trees; fill your home with candle scents, aromatherapy diffusers, and kitchen smells like apple crisp; follow your nose and wander toward farm smells, the musty essences of dark forests, and the scents of the sea; and accent holidays in purposeful aromas from Fourth of July barbecues and sparklers to roses and chocolates on Valentine's Day.

Isla Santa Magdalena, Baja California, Mexico

UNPLUG

The skies were rainy-gray, the winds strong and cold, yet we were willing to take a beating in the low-sided *panga* pounding through the rough waters of Magdalena Bay, for we all held visions of getting up close and personal with gray whales. They're gentle giants, in every sense of the word, annually migrating five thousand miles southward to these protected waters off the Pacific side of Baja California, Mexico, their winter nursery where they give birth and nourish their newborns with little fear from predators.

New life sparked our soggy spirits at the site of our first

"blow"——that miraculous rocketing mix of sea spray and life-giving breath signaling the surfacing of a whale. Our captain slowed the motor, cautiously approached a mom and calf serenely arching through the waters, and followed at a respectful distance until they tired of us. Their escape was an award-winning performance: ballet-graceful arcing into deep dives with a memorable finale, tail flukes rising cloudward with a showy "wave" goodbye before vanishing into the sea.

Suddenly the jagged silhouette of Isla Santa Magdalena, the site of our whale-watching base camp, appeared within the misty rain. When *el capitán* finally ran the *panga* up on the island's beach, we sat there for a stunned moment. Instead of the savvy safari tents we had imagined, a cluster of igloo-shaped tents squatted on this desolate, deserted desert isle, along with a MASH-type mess tent whose flat sunshade flapped in wild protest to the strength of the wind.

"Hop out and claim your tent," the captain said.

I jumped off and ran up the seashell-framed path winding around cacti armed in lethal-looking spikes and staked claim on the tent with an "ocean view" (the door flap faced the sea). It was roomy enough, with the thin red plastic covering the sandy floor weighted in place by rusting cots topped with rolled-up sleeping bags and clean sets of bed linens.

A bell echoed throughout the camp, summoning all to orientation: a tour of the two "comfort stations," each a tiny square stall with only three lemon-yellow plywood walls. Translation: a magnificent, unobstructed view of the mountains while in the most private of positions. The showers were short-hosed plastic bags filled with fresh water each morning and heated by the warmth of the sun. We were given a list of "always do's" like carrying flashlights at night for safe treading, and "never do's" like stashing food in tents or leaving anything outdoors that would tempt night-prowling coyotes to steal. No doubt about it, we were unplugged from the rest of the world in the strictest sense of the word.

Within a day, I had adapted to the island's effortless natural rhythms, rising with the bright orange sun languidly ascending from the water at the horizon, diffusing a promising hue over the base camp. Divine in both beauty and silence, it was a magical time to walk the cocoa-colored sands while everyone else still slept. With this early-morning taste of solitude wooing me (and the whales proving so elusive), I honored my inner call to stay behind, and bid *adios* to the rest of the whale watchers as they boarded the *pangas*—and thus fulfilled my lifelong fantasy of discovering whether being alone on a deserted island was, indeed, worth dreaming about.

Instead of the daily back-at-home ritual of sitting through life in front of some sort of screen or another, I found myself up and moving with the silent, powerful beat of the island, hiking and exploring mountain slopes where wildflowers, desert scrub, and cacti bloomed in wild, rugged beauty. I made my way up tow-ering *Lawrence of Arabia*–like sand dunes, scouting the tracks of coyotes, contemplating the easy glide of ospreys on the currents of the wind, relishing days alone barefoot and beachcombing at a lingering pace, discovering big purple barnacles, bright-orange scallop shells, lavender cones, and the biggest sand dollars I've ever seen.

The nature of this deserted *isla* teaches its own lessons: that sparse surroundings can be more nourishing than those of great abundance, that being disconnected from the world returns us to greater intimacy with ourselves, and that our days actually gain time when we simply pull the plug on intrusive distractions. It's well worth the leap into the unfamiliar and the risk of boredom, for it opens up unending possibilities and new ways of looking at life.

Being "unplugged" on Isla Santa Magdalena set me so glori-ously free of distraction that I could hardly contain myself. I re-claimed my ability to sense every moment, to act on natural impulses, and to unburden my mind. I could simply *be* without any dampening of spirit from bad news, pressure to do things, an-other's foul mood, or irreverent encroachments on my time. I felt completely in sync with life, reacquainted with my energy, filling time with only that which spoke to my heart. I took on a keen awareness of every little thing around me. Most important, I could hear myself think.

Every evening, when the whale watchers returned, we gathered in the mess tent, dining on cheesy *quesadillas* and Mexican-spicy fresh seafood, passing pitchers of homemade *margaritas*, singing "*La Bamba*" along with our guitar-playing cook, and dancing in the sand. As they eagerly shared tales of their quest for whale sightings, I sat silently with an inward smile, for I felt I had unearthed the true essence of Isla Santa Magdalena—the personal growth that comes from being alone, undaunted, and disconnected, and yet somehow more connected than ever before. Yes, it is worth dreaming of spending time on a deserted island, but even more valuable to pursue it.

DISCONNECT NOTICE

"It's distraction, not meditation, that becomes habitual; interruption, not continuity..." These words of author Tillie Olsen speak to a predicament most of us face. We have permitted irrelevant distractions to become some of our day's most unhealthy habits. They suck up the one precious commodity we're all so stressed out about—time—and take us far afield from the most meaningful things in life.

Intrusive distractions result in a mind-boggling inability to think things through and efficiently complete tasks, and to bestow uninterrupted attention on those we love. Think about it: the telephone rings, interrupting dinner with friends and family, the cell phone renders us incapable of simply having a relaxing cup of java, the beeper goes off while we're talking to a customer, an e-mail demands immediate attention, TV chatter consumes our evenings. The intrusive nature of the "e" (lectronic) life has taken over as the accepted, the expected, way of being.

More than any other time in the history of the world, we are weighted down by and entangled in so many visible and invisible electronic cords and cables that it feels as if we're always on the verge of short-circuiting. They are the ever-present meddlers, diverting us from what's important, cheating our good moods, arresting our enthusiasm, and detouring us from golden opportunities. They're akin to quicksand: we just sink deeper and deeper into their every-minute use, numbing ourselves to the world around us. We're so mired in distraction that we have forgotten that we do have a choice to live another way. We forget we can simply—pull the plug.

I have three friends who are TV free, only have cell phones for true emergencies, and rarely use computers at home. One has a house rule that between 5 and 8 P.M. the telephone is turned off to ensure uninterrupted family time. Another holds to a daily tradition in which she and her husband linger, uninterrupted, over a glass of wine on their front-porch swing before dinner, sharing the highs and lows of their day.

All three are up, out, and living, not the "e-life," but the "be-life." They're actually exercising, cooking, gardening, and traveling instead of watching others do it on TV; they seldom spend more than a few minutes on phone calls, and their children are outside playing instead of isolated in their rooms with machines. They're more in love with life than anyone else I know, always trying new things with great enthusiasm, meeting, accepting, and enjoying all kinds of people, approaching their days with vivid imagination. They're well read, culturally aware, and laugh a lot. They do not allow invasive distractions to alienate them from their own unique vision, and version, of life.

Maybe it's time we did the same, for without distractions taxing our time, energy, and concentration, everything from relationships to recreation takes on a whole new dimension; life, ideas, and opportunities will seem like they're on some magical roll. When we cut ourselves loose from cords of distraction, the tropical sky's the limit.

★ *Tune out.* Participate in TV Turnoff Week, sponsored by Washington, D.C.–based TV Turnoff Network, a growing movement in the U.S.A. They offer research and a newsletter with everything from "Tips for Turning Off" to "101 Screen-Free Activities" (www.tvturnoff.org).

★ *Unplug on vacation.* Leave the laptop, cell phone, and beeper at home so you can recharge within the ambiance of a relaxing lunch or intimate dinner, the theater, while driving, and on a real vacation. If you're plugged in while walking the beach or on the slopes, it's time to assess your addiction to distraction and distress.

⋆ *Courtesy call.* Use your cell phone only for emergencies, but if you can't break the habit, please use it with discretion and consideration for those around you who don't really want the distraction of your chatter or to know the intimacies of your problems. Remember that you got along just fine pre–cell phone.

⋆ *Don't be e-diverted.* It's easy to become ensnared by the wide array of activities and information on the Internet, but don't let yourself get hooked! Don't let the e-life divert you from what's truly important, from attaining your goals, allowing enough time to accomplish tasks, spending time with people you love, or being the best person you can be. Remember, the best form of learning doesn't come through a machine, but through the raw, immediate experience of life itself.

Chincoteague Island, Virginia

✴

UNWRAP THE GIFTS OF
YOUR ANCESTRY

Chincoteague Island has an old soul—and the cherished feel of hometown America where baseball and fishing are a normal part of the day, ruffled Priscilla curtains grace the windows of old Victorian homes, honesty and patriotism run flag-waving high, and mom-and-pop stores make shopping a family-warm encounter. Lying between Virginia's Eastern Shore and the barrier isle of Assateague Island, the island seduces adults longing to immerse themselves in this age-old "Chincoteague feel," as well as children who yearn to ride the descendants of the most popular little filly in children's literature, Misty of Chincoteague.

The book by the same name was authored by Marguerite Henry in 1946 and is still selling strong. Today visitors can still witness the annual Wild Pony Swim where the local herd is rounded up from their marshy grazing grounds on Assateague Island to swim across the channel to Chincoteague. It's one of those island traditions started in 1925 by early Teaguers (island borns) and, as with so many delights of island life here, hasn't changed much.

I couldn't help but feel that I was sharing the joys of earlier generations as I lounged on a backyard pier that stretched out over the shallow waters of the marshlands, eating sweet green figs a friend had just plucked off his tree, watching children polishing up their crabbing skills, and admiring flocks of geese as they flew into the magnificent colors of a setting sun. It's just the island thing to do, I was told.

Gathering on the screened porch of the old-fashioned ice cream parlor is another island thing to do. Here the Teaguers discuss the concerns of the community: the blessing of the fishing fleet, the defiant Civil War–era islanders who broke with the rest of Virginia and sided with the Yankees, how they're going to help a neighbor get the medicine he needs, and Ben Benson, a "come here" (nonlocal) treasure salvager who cruised in from the mainland one day in 1996 to test his new equipment before heading south in search of Caribbean wrecks. But Ben decided to drop anchor in Chincoteague all because of a local story.

As the Teaguers tell it, in 1802 a miracle sprung forth from a tragedy in the rough Atlantic waters off Assateague Island: a

Spanish galleon went down, sending everyone on board to a watery grave save for a three-year-old boy. Before vanishing beneath the sea, his mother, knowing her beloved young son had only one slim chance for survival, strapped him onto a hatch cover and set him adrift with a prayer on her lips and tears in her eyes.

The spirit of the sea did protect the child and directed the waves to deposit him on the shore of Assateague, where a couple found the frightened, olive-skinned boy who spoke a strange language. They named him James Alone and raised him as their own in the tiny village beneath the guiding light of the island's red-and-white-striped lighthouse.

The couple taught James the self-sufficient ways of the island's watermen: clamming, oystering, crabbing, shrimping, fishing, and living off the sea and the marshes. When he came of age, James rowed across the bay that separates Chincoteague from mainland Virginia, walked thirty miles to the courthouse, changed his last name to Lunn, returned to the island, and never left again.

The story drew me, like a magnet, to the ivory-colored sands of Assateague Island, where I sat, contented and alone, on the long peaceful stretch of pristine National Seashore where ponies run wild. I looked out over the white-capped waves of the Atlantic charging against the shoreline as I re-created the tale of the little boy's survival in my mind.

It's something Ernestine Holston, a native of Chincoteague whom I met during my travels there does often. She had heard the tale of James Alone from as early as she could remember, but it wasn't until she was twelve that her grandmother took her to the beach and showed her the place where the little boy was rescued, and told her about growing up on Assateague and how, in the early 1900s, the villagers had moved across the channel to Chincoteague Island because an absentee landowner had barred them from the clam flats.

She then took Ernestine home, handed the young girl an antiquated Bible, and from its aging pages took out a 1913 obituary printed on the stationery of J.T. Lunn & Sons, Planters and Packers of Fancy Oysters and Clams. It verified that J.T. Lunn's father, James (Alone) Lunn, had washed ashore as a little boy on the sands of Assateague and told the islanders that his son, J.T. had, ironically, died from drowning on April 11.

"That was how I learned where I came from," the bronze-skinned, dark-haired Ernestine told me. "I learned that I am the great-great-granddaughter of James Alone. I'm so proud of it! I'm so thankful to know where I come from. If it hadn't been for the survival of this little boy, I wouldn't be here. I consider it a miracle, don't you?"

Ernestine's late husband, John, was so fascinated by the story that he spent the last twenty years of his life researching the Lunn family tree and left, as part of his legacy to her, an enormous scroll with 350 names penned in his hand. More recently Ben Benson did go treasure hunting off the shores of Assateague Island and discovered a Spanish wreck, the *Juno,* the ship he believes carried the child into those waters. Now Benson is determined to trace the identity of James Alone's birth parents.

The combined research of Ben Benson and John Holston has shown that about 25 percent of the 3,500 people of Chincoteague Island can trace their roots to James Alone. Most have bronze skin and dark hair, and all are proud of their ancestry. These are the "Mediterranean Chincoteaguers," all sharing history and Lunn traits; all connected because of one child's unyielding sense of survival.

Sharing prevails on Chincoteague to this day: the whole island is like one big family, whether you are called Savage, Bunting, Whealton, Lunn, or any of the other pioneering family names. Or even if you're a "come here." No one ever goes hungry; if someone gets sick or down on his luck, everyone jumps in to help—just like the couple who took James Alone into their home. It was the way of their ancestors, and it still triumphs today.

IT'S ALL RELATIVE

Delving into our ancestry can be a rewarding adventure with all the suspense of solving a good mystery. It's a journey of discovery, of searching out clues, of rendezvousing with compelling or entertaining characters who have, in some way or another, shaped who we are.

That's where, in my book, the fun lies, for who can resist the alluring possibility of being kin to the likes of royalty, scoundrels or cowboys, intellectuals or shamans, artists or playwrights, or even rebels without a cause? In familiarizing ourselves with our ancestors we discover whose blood courses through our veins, what influences our shared DNA brings into our character and into our health, what basic truths of life and love live on in our ancestral wisdom, and what hidden, handed-down traits or talents may be waiting for just the right moment to make their appearance.

Getting acquainted with our forebears—their names, origins, what they were made of, what they were all about, the strength of their constitution—is akin to acknowledging, and maybe even discovering, a part of who we are in a more intimate, detailed way. Sometimes our lineage brings to light the whys and wherefores of things we haven't been able to fully understand, like why we're so different from the rest of our family. With just a bit of research we may discover that we're just one wonderful chip off a great-aunt's block, one who was a bit more defiant, independent, or just had a different take on life. By unearthing a kindred spirit in our family tree, we complete the puzzle and find a sense of belonging, in spite of our differences.

Since the United States is such a young country, we, as Americans, don't have to look too far back to uncover great deeds and daring choices in our past. Most of us can easily discover someone who courageously fought for the freedom and values our country stands for in one of the world wars, who bravely followed the call of "Westward, ho!" and moved on past the Mississippi River into dangerous and unknown territory, or who left their homeland and immigrated to America in search of a better life. These choices of our forebears have greatly impacted who, and what, we are, and the freedoms we enjoy as Americans today. By taking the time to acquaint ourselves with our personal histories we gain an appreciation of what we have been given. It reminds us that we, too, will leave a legacy for generations ahead.

* *Story time.* Sit down with the oldest members of your distant, as well as immediate, family and, as the Hawaiians say, "Talk story." You'll be surprised what surfaces once the memories start rolling. Remember, also, to share the stories of your own life with others. Most important, record every word everyone says—and pass it on.

* *Ances-tree.* Researching your genealogy is more popular, and easier, than ever before. The Family History Library of the Church of Jesus Christ of Latter-Day Saints in Salt Lake City, offers free daily introductory classes to get your family tree started, plus a wealth of records (800-537-5950). Look to lo-

cal library genealogy departments and local clubs whose members are more than happy to help. The Internet has websites galore (be cautious of the accuracy of some); try www.cyndislist.com.

★ *Surround yourself with the spirits of your ascendants.* Feel a grandmother's loving embrace each time you wrap yourself in her handmade quilt; a pot of tea steeped in your aunt's teapot resurrects thoughts of her dancing eyes as she served warm plum pie topped with homemade ice cream; a granddad's baseball cap always brings on the spirit of loving hugs. These moments add more to the day than you're ever aware of.

★ *Don't throw away your past.* Resist the urge to throw away old photographs. Instead, allow them to bring your family together with a common purpose. Plan an evening of fun going through boxes of old photos and discuss, speculate, and have a good time. Give some away to those who'll value them; paste them on (or insert them in) note cards and mail to other family members to remind them of your ancestral traditions and those who came before.

Terceira, the Azores, Portugal

✳

CREATE FESTIVITY

"Festivities make people happy," a Terceiran told me while sipping a tiny cup of strong Portuguese coffee in a *pastelarias* (pastry shop). "We love to be happy. When you live on a powder keg, you never tire of celebrating life."

That "powder keg" is the topography of the Azores, nine endearing islands isolated in the deep Atlantic between North America and Europe, with a long history of plundering pirates, earthquakes, and lava-spewing volcanoes. Over centuries, these forces have wrought havoc on the lives, the homes, and the fields of the Azoreans, who have naturally come to possess souls that thrive on poetry, music, dance—and festivity.

Each of the villages within the islands has its own signature recipe for celebrating the festivities named mostly in honor of saints, but it's Terceira, "the happy island," that has a special reputation for nurturing the innate impulse to have fun. So whole communities gather together like one big family for over a hundred festivities a year to share the pleasure of traditions and diversions, Terceira-style: a miraculous union of a religion, antiquated customs of the agrarian calendar, and just out-and-out good times. The Terceirans render each festivity, in the words of poet Alexander Pope, "a feast of reason and the flow of soul."

I was thrilled to be invited to join the villagers in the revered *Festas do Espírito Santo* (Holy Spirit Celebration), standing on an ancient street of black cobblestone cut from lava rock in the city of Angra do Heroísmo (a gorgeous UNESCO World Heritage Site). We all watched the traditional procession led by children dressed as if for first communion and adults wearing their Sunday finest as they carried ornate, antique silver crowns of all sizes, gleaming in the sunlight, the grand symbol of the popular *festa*.

The processioners solemnly made their way to the cathedral, serenaded by the local *filharmonic*, a 105-year-old marching band bringing up the rear. The spectators filed in behind them, flowing into the crowded church for a Mass highlighted by the crowning of the "emperor" who has taken on much of the responsibility of carrying out the traditions of the *festa*.

Around the corner, in front of the *império* (an ornate, tiny chapel-style building where the crowns are displayed enveloped in white flowers), my heart was both touched and impressed by a perfectly straight line of end-to-end tables stretching for block after block, beautifully set for over two hundred people.

Here the inhabitants of the city sit down family-style, under the clear Azorean sky, to enjoy each other and the ancestral feast: pitchers of *vinho de cheiro* (the local red wine), *sopa Espírito Santo* (Holy Ghost soup), *cozido* (platters of meat), a never-ending supply of breads including the sweet *massa sovada* and lots of rice pudding for dessert. It is an all-you-can-eat kind of affair, an example of the generous nature of the locals, after which the solemnity of religion quickly gives way to a rousing good time.

The revelry goes on for days, accented by nostalgic pageantry and featuring feasting, folkloric costumes, singing, dancing, and live music, including the fifteen-string guitar unique to Terceira (a pure delight to listen and dance to), Terceira-style bull fighting in the streets, with a bull on a rope, lavish flower adornments placed on calves before they're sacrificed to feed the poor (even though there really are no poor anymore), and all of the villagers participating with high spirits.

People live close to the earth here and a devoted sense of community prevails based on the three virtues of Azorean culture taught through age-old rituals: equality (everyone is middle class and embraces an "anyone can do it" attitude), fraternity (within equality everyone is like a brother or a sister), and generosity (it's only right to share what you have with your brothers and sisters). This wonderfully comforting take on life doesn't stop there, for if a stranger, like me, appears in the country, villagers insist that you eat with them, even if they've never laid eyes on you before, and their warmth and openness is something I'll never forget.

The goal of all Azoreans is to live a good life. They don't seek riches; everyone is honest and trusting and expects honesty in return; they revere the wisdom of elders and ancient customs. Life is calm, guided by etiquette and doctrine and lived without crime amid people of good character in caring little communities where friendships are strong.

"We have to have time," an educator told me, "quality time to do what's important like going home and having lunch, time with family, to create, to sing, to open our windows and stare out at the island and the sea. This is priceless. This is what we like to do."

Businesses close at noon on Saturdays and don't open again until Monday morning; of course, they're closed for festivities, too. There's time for working hard, but it's always balanced with making time to duck into favorite little spots for an espresso or *galão* (coffee with milk served in a tall glass) and island talk, to swim in the protected, natural pools of the sea formed by a lava flow of many years ago, to play volleyball, to dance in folkloric groups, to sing, to play the land guitars and mandolins, to practice embroidery, to play cards—and, of course, to plan and partake in festivities.

"It's just the spirit here," a Terceiran said. In my view it's the "holy spirit," a saintly sensation that enhances a simple formula for adding a divine Midas touch to the pleasures of daily life.

FESTIVE-FULL

It's natural to view life through festive colored sunglasses when we live with the uncertainty of a volcano blowing. Time takes on new definition—we become determined to make every moment count in the most important of ways; and time itself becomes something we look forward to, to be enjoyed, rather than something we're always butting our heads against. We purposefully take steps to inject it with special people, things we love to do, and great food. Good times become an island-wise priority.

We don't need a volcano breathing down our neck to know that, no matter where we live, life can change in an instant, so the Terceirans' infatuation with creating fun days is something we all need to take to heart. In fact, we owe it to ourselves, and those around us, to make the time we have on this earth feel full, beautiful, stimulating, and, yes, festive. Festive time can often prevent our own volcanoes from erupting—anger and resentment, stress and tension, grumpiness and grouchiness, and the heaviness that burdens our days.

Cultivating a flair for festivity is simply about releasing a spirit already yearning to create a sense of excitement for living and glorifying our days with fun, amusement, celebration. To embrace a festive spirit is to paint our time with bold, showy brushstrokes of vivid, colorful, and positive emotions, high-spirited music, little (but extraordinary) touches, and any reason (serious to frivolous) to give birth to those joyful sensations that rescue us from boredom and lackluster and listless living.

Just think creatively with a pinch of whimsy thrown in. Let ease and simplicity be your guides and remember there are a zillion reasons for coaxing your mood right into a festive spirit—for example, Mick Jagger's birthday. Just pick up a cake and candles, put on some Stones tunes, strut your stuff, make a wish for Mick, and eat cake!

Anything can inspire festive moods and become the subject of joyous times. All it took in Terceira was a look to the saints calendar and a whole year of communal festivities found its reason. On Tortola in the British Virgin Islands, a local named Bomba looked up at the sky one night and, voila! his famous full-moon parties were born. When a few Hawaiians were stirred by the ancient hula, the ever-popular Merry Monarch Festival got its start, and when a guy named Murphy, sitting in a Kansas City bar on St. Patrick's Day, talked his comrades into parading through the streets, he gave birth to one of the grandest St. Patty's Day parades in the States.

All it takes is the idea of one person with a festive nature and, suddenly, the world takes on a lighter, more fun-flavored feel.

So unleash your imagination, take the initiative, and realize that you have the power to sculpt life with joy and laughter. When you cultivate a Terceira kind of devotion to celebrating life, you brighten the landscape for everyone around you.

☆ *Plan weekly food festivities.* Food is one of the simplest, most enjoyable ways to bring people together. Schedule a chocolate night and indulge in fun things like fondue, the best truffles in town, brownies. Reserve Friday nights for macaroni and cheese, ice cream, and Monopoly, or Sundays for breakfast picnics where you cook up bacon and eggs in the fresh air of a park, followed by a nature walk.

☆ *Celebrate everything!* Look to *The World Almanac* or *Chase's Calender of Events* for fun dates to transform into occasions, like Bogey and Bacall's wedding anniversary, Hemingway's birthday, Armstrong's walk on the moon, the shoot-out at the OK Corral, a saint's day that carries your name—the possibilities are endless.

☆ *Decorate your life!* Colorful paper lanterns, strings of lights that look like pineapples or flamingoes, flaming tiki torches. Eating by candlelight, blowing a conch shell instead of ringing a dinner bell. These fun little touches can create a perky atmosphere any time of the year.

★ *Fashion fest.* Nothing sets a lighter frame of mind than what you choose to wear. Your clothes, and your accessories, can spark up your self-image, can invite you to feel brighter, jauntier, and more joyful. How you feel about the way you look can divert your thoughts to fun and play, and thus free up a spontaneity that delivers you to unplanned stops for sunset cocktails or lunches with a special touch. So get out those bright-colored beads, shimmery earrings, ultrafeminine shawls and enjoy their festive influences on your psyche.

Borneo

THE HEART OF COURTESY

Borneo is wild and wonderful and it makes travelers feel the same way. This island of mystery, magic, and marvel struck a chord deep within my soul and awoke many of the characters who dwell within me. The neglected adventurer came alive while cruising down muddy rivers in small, slightly leaking, *pangas* to spy on probiscus monkeys hanging out in mangrove trees. The nature lover was struck with awe by the craggy, snow-topped peak of Mount Kinabalu and the jungle-lush rain forests brushed in greens of every imaginable hue, accented by the Christmas-red trunks of lipstick palms and orchids of every color and size. The beachcomber relished solitary walks along the surfline where water buffaloes basked lazily while the South China Sea kissed the golden sands of Rasa Ria. And the romantic exploded onto the scene (à la Dorothy Lamour) when I swapped my khaki shorts and blouse for the mandatory batik sarong at a remote lodge built of bamboo and secreted within thick wilds where elephants roamed.

But it was the orangutans, those orangey red—haired primates once dubbed the "wild men of Borneo" who brought out the softy in me. These endangered wonders (who share 94 percent of our DNA) have always held a special place in my heart, but I became hooked for life when I felt the warm, gentle hand of a mother, with a wide-eyed precious little orphaned baby clinging to her back, tapping against my bare leg, her courteous way of asking me to move aside so they could continue on their path through the Sepilok Orangutan Sanctuary.

That same surprising gentleness not only showed through the untamed wilderness, but was an integral part of the cities and fishing villages built on stilts above the water. It springs from a tribal island culture where respect, regard, and courtesy toward one another is at the very heart of their code of conduct.

While touring the state of Sabah, I noticed the Sabahans greeting everyone they encountered with wide, dancing eyes, the sincerest of smiles, and a boundless consideration for one another. Masters at extending courtesy, they truly believe that, no matter who you are or where you come from, everyone deserves thoughtful attention. I watched as Ross, my English-speaking guide through the countryside, addressed everyone we met along the way with kind, gentle words.

"It's our custom," Ross explained, "to respect everyone. We address anyone older than ourselves as Uncle or Aunt like 'Uncle Elias' or 'Aunt Tulip,' even if they're not related to us. Someone our own age, or younger, we call 'Brother John' or 'Sister Claudine.' Without courtesy, our culture would fall apart. It guides our behavior. We always think twice when tempted to misbehave or do something wrong. We always think about our choices, our actions, because we would never intentionally bring disgrace upon our parents. Nor would we want to disgrace ourselves."

Pride flashed across Ross's face as he told me about meeting his fiancée in the checkout lane of a local store and about his adherence to his village's customary route to the altar. His uncle spoke to his fiancée's father to approve the union, and together they set the dowry: one water buffalo plus five hundred dollars. So he's a busy guy these days, making and saving as much money as he can, but not only for the dowry. The responsibility of the wedding, which the whole village attends, falls on his shoulders, as well as the cost for his tribal wedding costume. Since he's an avid conservationist, he's also scouring the forests in his spare time, searching for the impressive feathers dropped by the hornbill bird so he can make his tribe's traditional wedding headdress.

"I'm also saving for a house for us to live in," he said.

"Is it easy to get a mortgage here?" I asked.

"Oh, I would never think of going into debt for our home," he said a little surprised at my question. "That would not be a courteous way to enter a marriage. So we won't be getting married for two years. That's OK, though. That's the way we do things."

As we drove on, our eyes searching trees for hornbill birds perched on branches, I looked over at Ross, with his gentle disposition and heart-melting smile. It had been a long while since I had felt such admiration for someone who held courtesy, concern for others, and traditional values more important than his own selfish desires, who was willing to work so hard toward his dream and patiently wait for his money to accumulate rather than go into debt. But then that's just expected as the courteous thing to do in Borneo.

PUT YOUR BEST FOOT FORWARD

The Sabahans' gracious treatment of each other reminds me of the courting stage of romantic relationships back home, when everything is new and exciting and we're determined to put our best foot forward. Our goal is to treat each other with the highest regard, and consideration, politeness, and attentiveness are at the forefront of our behavior. We mind our manners, watch our language, and strive to make each other feel special; we offer the

gift of courtesy all wrapped up in the ribbons of our own individual spirit of giving our best.

But then we let familiarity supersede consideration as the relationship continues. Too much of the time we neglect opportunities to extend consideration to others simply because we're
moving too fast through life, focusing on everything except the
present moment. We're unaware of, and unable to connect with,
the subtleties of each encounter—its true meaning, its emotion,
its activity, its needs, and its possibilities. Each moment offers a
choice: to be thoughtful or to be thoughtless. We can make others feel either valued, complimented, and joyous or undervalued,
degraded, and deflated.

I learned all about thoughtful choices and courtesy at the
Sandakan fish market, where I faced my own inability to recognize the kindnesses shown to me. It's a wonderful, lively place to
mingle with locals carrying out their daily routine. The fish boats
are tied up to the dock, where the captain and crew transfer their
fresh catches into the traditional hand-woven baskets to be carried to the icy tables of the fishmongers.

I strolled around, caught up in the excitement of activity, listening to the noisy haggling over the fish and peeking into baskets brimming with eels and stingrays, shellfish and shark, and
other sea creatures I'd never seen before. The vendors, ranging
from whole families to groups of young men, hailed me with en-
thusiastic grins, offering themselves as subjects for my photos, an
unusually openhearted gesture. But since the market is not well

lit and I, unfortunately, had left my flash locked up in the van, I thoughtlessly declined each courteous invitation without realizing how I had dishonored the people who had graciously offered me a favor.

Later, as I sat outside on the dock savoring the novel taste of juicy rambutans I had just purchased from a fruit vendor, I was struck by a haunting flashback—the downcast eyes of people whose kindness I had rebuffed. My thoughtless "no" was an indignity to my own spirit as well; I felt terrible. In the end, I returned to all of the vendors who had offered me a photo op and took their pictures. Smiles returned, good feelings were restored for all of us, honor, respect and courtesy were reestablished. I had recovered my opportunity to respond with grace.

Courtesies are powerful gifts which can easily be given; spreading courtesy is akin to circulating a good mood. Spirits and self-worth soar with just a mere whisper of a compliment, or the opening of a door, or the discovery of a piece of pie a neighbor left on the step. There are silent courtesies, too: prayers, thoughts of good luck, and positive affirmations sent to one another.

The universe is forever inviting us to make the world be a better place to live, and we need to stop overlooking opportunities to put our best foot forward, to add to rather than detract from the encounter, and to put value into each and every experience. Courtesy in most mainland worlds seems to be as endangered as Borneo's orangutans. Children grow up watching nightly sitcoms and Saturday morning shows whose dialogue is rooted in sarcasm, put-downs, and degradation. The "in" lingo within too many families and between friends and coworkers is sarcasm and profanity. Teens call their parents vulgar names and think nothing of it, employers talk to their employees in degrading tones, even our doctors have fallen into discourteous disregard of their patients in the name of professionalism and efficiency. It just doesn't feel good—or right.

Common courtesy is more than simply treating others as you wish they'd treat you, it is the antithesis of indifference. Harry S Truman once said, "We must build a new world, a far better world—one in which the eternal dignity of man is respected." And it can happen if, one by one, we call upon our spiritual etiquette, those little acts of connection and kindness that so positively influence the soul of mankind.

★ *Don't be rude.* Consideration of others requires only common sense. Think twice—before you talk through a movie in a theater, before you hog all the shrimp cocktail at a brunch buffet, before you show impatience with another in a checkout line merely because that person needs a moment to put away change. It's just a matter of considerate behavior.

★ *Mind your manners.* The world feels the loss of these wonderful little pleasantries that symbolize respect. Let's bring back greetings and niceties like "good morning," "please," "thank you," "you're welcome," and "excuse me." Let's revive outward respect for elders and authority with the use of "Mr.," "Mrs.," or "Miss." Let's make gracious, kind behavior the "in" conduct of the day.

* *Turn off sources of negativity.* Turn off the crude sitcoms, and music with lyrics that send indecent, tasteless, and brutal messages. Crack down on sarcasm and profanity in your home by demanding more respect for each other.

* *Be courteous to yourself.* Think more of yourself than to accept discourteous treatment from anyone. If someone is always putting you down, treating you in a degrading manner, or ignoring your needs, call them on it. Set limits as to what behavior you'll accept from others, and set goals of only allowing those who court courtesy into your life.

Cuba

☀

FOLLOW LIFE'S RHYTHMS

V iva el mojito!" is written along with the autographs of Ernest Hemingway and Fidel Castro on the walls of Old Havana's La Bodeguita del Medio, the most famous bar in the world in which to sip the most famous of Cuban cocktails: the *mojito*, the refreshing combination of fresh mint and local rum.

La Bodeguita is a Caribbean hole-in-the-wall, shiftless in character, and subtly sultry and sensual in a raw kind of way. Often one of the local guitar players will drop in and dole out traditional musical instruments to guests and revelers, sparking a collaborative frenzy of Cuban music that builds to rousing heights. Before I knew it, I was rattling a *chequeré* (a gourd covered in beads) alongside others clicking *claves* (wooden sticks), shaking *maracas,* and banging on *bongos.*

It's easy to get caught up in the exhilaration of Cuba's bold rhythms. So the island-happy tourists will generously tip the guitarist in U.S. dollars, the most valuable of the country's three currencies. His smile contains an undercurrent of relief: with the extra money he'll be able to supplement his family's meager monthly food ration, perhaps adding a little meat to the normally meatless table. He might also be able to round up scarce household basics like toilet paper, or treat his eight-year-old daughter to a glass of milk—or possibly an ice cream cone. He stashes the dollars in his pocket and quietly slips away, for islanders are generally forbidden in tourist establishments—there are even doormen to ensure they stay away. Even if they were welcome, a local could never enjoy a three-dollar *mojito*—that's about one eighth of a doctor's monthly salary.

Welcome to Cuba, a fascinating, enigmatic, deeply romantic, and tragic country. At first glance, the capital city of Havana could be mistaken for a Hollywood movie set, with its old, crumbling buildings, pretty little *plazas,* colorful street performers, book vendors, and entire families piled onto Urals (Russian copies of earlier-era BMW motorcycles) with side cars scooting down the streets. The Urals share the roads with chrome-gleaming American cars from the forties and fifties (from Studebakers to Chevys) smoothed over with Bondo to hide the rust, brightly colored and some now powered by Russian diesel engines when their tires aren't flat. Even though the vehicles are packed with people, they stop to pick up hitchhikers on their way to work. And when there's a breakdown, the men, probably the best mechanics in the world, lift the hoods, creatively invent solutions (spare parts are rare), and get the cars up and running in record time—an example of the ingenuity, resiliency, and strength of spirit of the Cubans. When they encounter obstacles—and there are many in this decaying communist outpost—they don't complain, but instead ask "how can I make this work?"

"People seem happy here," I commented to a local.

"Ah, yes," he said, "But 'seem' is the key word. Look beyond the smile."

A disturbing sense of repression, the subduer of the soul, lies beneath those Cuban smiles. It casts a somber shadow on everyone and everything, except the ephemeral tropical-island mood that tourists get swept away in. The locals have to be cautious about what they say aloud, and where they say it, for here there's no freedom of speech. All take great pride in speaking the English they learn through a very good school system, but were quick to tell me there's little, if any, opportunity for their education to improve their lot in life once they graduate. But, in spite of the goal of equality within the country's communist doctrine, a class system is developing: those who receive tips (in U.S.

dollars) from travelers, who work in tourism, or as beggars are the "have a little mores" and those in professions that don't receive tips, such as physicians or teachers are "the have a little lesses."

Gone are the exciting tastes of Cuban cuisine, even in the tourist restaurants, for the ingredients are simply unavailable. The locals receive monthly rations, an ever-boring menu dominated by beans, rice, and eggs, except for the meat they receive once, maybe twice, a year, and they have to boil their drinking water daily to avoid stomach problems, a statement in itself on the status of the island's infrastructure. Equally heartbreaking is the deterioration of Havana's lavish old-world architecture, which once rivaled that of Paris. It has fallen into disrepair, crying out for paint and restoration, but the materials aren't available, except through a few European investors who, partnered with the Cuban government, have recently rescued some old gems, restoring them as hotels. And those famous hand-rolled Cuban cigars? Breathe easy. Their odor is scarce because the locals can't afford them.

Nevertheless, the dispiriting lack of everything from freedom and opportunity to milk and variety in life seems to fade at the first beat of a Cuban tune, whether the rhythm dives into an island-born rumba, mambo, cha-cha, salsa, or son. The islanders' eyes light up, their longing to feel good takes over, passions rise and they are in every sense of the word, liberated, free to sway their hips, free to sing and shake *maracas*, free to become one with the music, and free to be themselves.

"Music is life to us," my tour guide, Oti, said as he danced down the sidewalk with the first smile I saw on his face all day.

The music echoes through the air all of the time, everywhere—in the cities, the countryside, and the mountains—from the soulful, haunting sound of a solo sax player leaning against a doorway in the cool air of a dimly lit night, to neighborhood jams trying out the unique beat of Cuban rap, to the pros who draw standing-room-only crowds (inside and out) at the Café Paris. Within the potent, lusty beats of the *tumbadora* (conga drums), *maruga* (metal shakers), *guiro* (an elongated gourd scraped with a stick), and *claves*, everything else in life is forgotten. The music, the beat, the dance, and the person become one—and hope is kindled. They feel the song that lives in their souls and they dance out the emotions that dwell in their hearts. Just for a little while, everything feels so good, and so free.

MUSICAL NOTES

It's hard to imagine the world without music. It's the universal language that connects us all on an emotional level. It delivers us from apathy, acts as our muse, and often gives us the enlightening sense that what's bad in our life really isn't as bad as we think, and that the good is even better. Music is potent medicine, restorative and healing, enabling us, regardless of who we are or where we live, to soar up to the higher notes of life. It takes us back to better times, eases desperation, helps us work through sorrows, and charges up our energy; it can make us whole when we feel fragmented. Music seeps deep inside of us, into those secret pockets of our inner self and touches us where, and when, nothing else can.

When we listen to music, we find, like the islanders of Cuba, our hips begin to play, our shoulders shimmy, our voices sing out. We stand taller and vitality is injected into our steps. The rhythm of life swells within us—a primal response, and a remedy for what ails us, one that shamans and healers have turned to for thousands of years.

Scientists tell us that different kinds of music stimulate different parts of our brain. For example, classical music, particularly Mozart, has been found to relieve stress, improve memory, shorten learning time, increase efficiency, acclerate healing, calm hyperactive children, and spark creativity. Music also encourages higher rates of data retention, which improve students' test scores. It stimulates plants to grow better, and a Japanese sake brewery found that serenading fermenting rice wine produced their best sake. The Canadian city of Edmonton plays classical music to calm pedestrians in crowded areas, and at a Baltimore hospital, the director of the coronary care unit reported that a half hour of Mozart produces the same effect as ten milligrams of Valium. Author Don Campbell has written about these benefits as the Mozart Effect.

But we needn't limit our choices to classical; it's been proven that all different kinds of music are beneficial. We simply need to listen to what speaks to our needs and our moods of the moment: the playfulness of Little Richard's rock and roll, that down-and-dirty feel of rhythm and blues, that cry-in-our-beer country and western sound, the free flow of a waltz, or the unplugged, yet potent rhythms of Cuba driven by hand-drumming, the heartbeat of their music. Perhaps it is that heartlike thumping, so much like that of our own hearts, that holds the secret to music's power to reawaken us to the beauty of being alive.

---

* *Go live*. Set aside one day a week for a live-music encounter, whether it's a jazz jam at a local bar, the performance of a symphony, a musical play, singing in the church choir, a family night sing-a-long, or a drumming circle on the beach at sunset.

* *Move while you groove*. Music and dance are perfect partners. According to the Mayo Clinic, dancing can burn as many calories as walking, swimming, or riding a bicycle (and it's a lot more fun!). So put on some energetic music, go for a half hour of sustained, high-spirited dancing and burn 200–400 calories while brightening your day.

* *Serenade your day*. No matter what kind of day you're having, listening to music will make it better.

Instead of settling in for an evening of uninspiring TV, pop in the CDs, sing along, and take a few lighthearted spins around the living room floor. There's nothing quite so powerful or uplifting as voices raised in song.

Baranoff Island,
Alaska

GIVE BACK

With the sun's rays reflecting off its waters like a million dancing diamonds, Sitka Sound carried me away, with secluded homes secreted in the deep-green spruce forests of its pretty little cluster of islets, and kayakers slowly paddling along a backdrop of larger-than-life mountains whose craggy summits are painted in blinding-white snow. Baranoff Island exudes a uniqueness of soul, as if it were the keeper of divine knowledge; the land emanates the essence of sacred ground. It's no wonder, this is the ancestral home of the Kinsadi clan of Tlingits, the artistic native people of southeast Alaska, who have lived in, and cared for, this ethereal part of the earth for over fifteen thousand years.

Sitka, once the capital of Russian America, exudes an "authentic town" feel these days, with a thriving Ben Franklin five-and-dime, an old-fashioned drug store, and a couple of restaurants serving satisfying comfort food. Totem Park, the town's square, is dominated by totem poles, intricately hand-carved long ago by the Tlingits, a people who have always held Mother Earth, and all of her life, in reverence, taking only what they truly need, wasting nothing, and always giving back in some form.

This vital element of clan life goes back eons and touches upon everything they do, including fishing for wild salmon, which has always kept them so well fed that their language has never known a word for starvation. For millennia they have made their way to the undisturbed islands of the Inside Passage and set up fish camps, their base where the catch was dried, and thus preserved. At night they would lie down under ink-black skies lit by bright stars and the Northern Lights, those flowing brush strokes of colors, like neon chartreuse, which sweep the sky in beautiful abstracts. The lyrical sounds of nature lulled them to sleep: the lapping water, the exhalations of humpback whales surfacing for air, the last barkings of sea lions before they succumbed to slumber, and the godlike "white thunder," the native term for the boisterous groanings of thousand-year-old glaciers colored an unbelievable ice blue.

When the fishing began, the bones of the first salmon caught were (and still are) ceremoniously given back to the waters to reproduce and return the next year, for the Tlingits have always believed they are one with the earth and that everything from the wind to the rocks possesses a spirit deserving of respect.

"If you take, if you receive, you must give something back," John Bell, a Tlingit with straight raven-black hair reaching almost to his waist, told me. "It's at the heart of our culture. It keeps our community balanced."

The Raven and Eagle clans of Sitka strive to adhere to their tribe's philosophy on life by continuing to hold potlatches in the oldest active clan house in Alaska. These intricate, elaborate ceremonial gatherings are focused on restoring balance to all. It's a time when they pay back those who have given something to their life, to settle debts, to support and alleviate the grieving of those whose loved ones have passed on.

The dayslong ceremony ends in a finale of ancient chants in the Tlingit language, powerful beats of deerskin drums, and joyous dancing to spread happiness. Clan members of all ages, from infants to elders, are dressed in traditional regalia: ceremonial robes of black and red with their family crest outlined in beadwork or mother-of-pearl buttons, and crowned in intricate headdresses like the *shakee.at* (hand-carved, accented in ermine, and "tipped in sea lion whiskers, which shimmer and shake when the wearer's head snaps to the beat of the drum").

It was the joyous dances, chants, and drumming of the potlatches the Sheet'ka Kwaan Naa Kahidi Dancers performed

181

around a fire in the clan house that sparked one of those inexplicable emotional releases in me. When they offered the invitation, I found myself up and dancing with them around the fire, tears streaming from my eyes.

"What happened to me?" I asked John later.

"It's a force—a spirit. If you're open enough, you become connected. If you reach out, you'll receive it. I guess you received it."

"How do you say thank you in Tlingit?" I asked.

"*Gunalcheesh*," he said.

"*Gun-al-cheesh*," I tried to repeat.

"You just gave back to the spirit." John said. "It's as simple as that."

RECIPROCAL PRIVILEGES

Reciprocity is defined as a mutual exchange of privilege. The Tlingits hold this mutual exchange, this taking and giving, as an exchange of spirit. It's an important balancing act that we need to revive, as it affects so many aspects of our own lives: our relationships, our awareness of kindnesses, favors, and beauty injected into our lives, their worth to us, and what kind of people we are, self-serving or benevolent.

We seem to be living in an age of take, take, take, accumulating so much more than we could ever need that it all loses purpose and value. We take from those close to us and too often forget to hug a little tighter, smile a little bigger, or even whisper simple words of gratitude. Our business dealings forge ahead without note as to whether they take advantage of another, use up resources that belong to every single being on earth, or destroy the essence of a community. Mother Earth's life-sustaining blessings—the air we breathe, the water we drink, the food that keeps us healthy, and the land where we build our shelter—are all taken for granted without acting to heal the wounds that we inflict.

Any relationship, whether it be with a loved one, a colleague, a customer, a neighbor, or the earth, works best when it's in a state of balance, when an interchange of effort, of love, of acknowledgment and appreciation create a partnership of equals. For when well-planned gifts go unnoticed by the receiver, when a little extra-something given by a loving spouse goes ignored, when a special picture drawn by a child gets lost in a pile of unread magazines, it leaves a haunting, hurt feeling in the heart of the giver.

Reciprocity introduces three powerful forces into our lives: the balance the Tlingits so wisely value, a consciousness of what we receive, and the creation and dissemination of positive energy in the form of gratitude. It's a dynamic force that must be allowed to complete its full cycle, a circle of inflowing and outflowing energy, for it to achieve its full, positive potential.

If we gracefully compliment those who have added to our day by writing a quick e-mail to say thank you, cook up a spouse's favorite meal, pay back money loaned to us in a time of need, treat our coworkers with extra gratitude and consideration for the work they do, or bake a cake to thank a friend for being there when we needed a shoulder to cry on, we create a win-win situation for all, and we perpetuate the goodness.

To do this, we need to identify the instances when we are recipients of positive efforts, recognize them as having great value, and take pride in giving back with a show of appreciation. The whole experience will feel more full and complete. Taking and giving back go together like peanut butter and jelly; they complement each other, elevating the best of each of us to a more gracious level.

Since my time on Baranoff Island, I have incorporated a "receive and reciprocate" philosophy in my life. For example, every morning when I beachcomb and pick up seashells and sand dollars, I also pick up the trash others have left behind. When my mother worries about me, I thank her for the intense love at the core of her panic, and when my husband works so hard to make our life better, I reciprocate with back rubs and antics to make him laugh. And each evening, I thank the universe for everything positive that has come my way. Mutual exchange is a natural part of keeping the world in a state of harmony. If the wisdom of the Tlingits were practiced by everyone, what a wonderful world it could be.

✳ *Revive thank-you notes.* To sit down and write an old-fashioned hand-written thank-you note for kindnesses bestowed upon us reminds us that someone out there holds us in their hearts; to open the mailbox and find a thank-you note always brings on a wonderful glow because we know we have touched another person's life. Make it a practice, then sit down and teach it to your children.

✳ *Keep a gratitude journal.* Follow the advice of *Simple Abundance* author Sarah Ban Breathnach and keep a gratitude journal. You'll be a lot more aware of the beauty and kindnesses that have come your way and, thus, be more appreciative of the people and things that enrich your life.

✳ *Impart from the heart.* A gift given with "good turn" sentiment means a thousandfold more than when we quickly charge a present at a store. Instead of buying an impersonal gift or tchotchke, try giving a plate of homemade cookies, a bouquet of flowers cut from your own garden, a sack of oranges picked from your backyard tree, or a big pot of chicken soup you've simmered with love.

✳ *Thank the blues away.* Offer a prayer of gratitude when you want to feel the high of reciprocity during the day. You may discover that your saying "thank you" a lot, which can override feelings of having a bad day. Thus, feelings of frustration, anger, stress, or sorrow can be quelled by the positive might of gratitude.

Jost Van Dyke, the British Virgin Islands

✺

STEAL IDLE MOMENTS

No matter how many times I sail the British Virgin Islands, I never tire of them. The laid-back breeze simply blows away the cares and worries of all us "yachties"—mainlanders turned sea gypsies—chartering sailboats out of Tortola, our course set for the great escape where there's "nahting to tink about" but the direction of the wind. Because "nahting" else matters at the moment, mon. It's that simple.

The British Virgin Islands are an isle-o-phile's dream—a scattering of fun islands, lime green and hilly, sitting atop deep turquoise waters teeming with sailboats, their sails filled with tropical wind and flying freely like big white butterflies. Beach bars line the shore, serving up rosy-red fruit punches, spicy conch fritters, a reggae beat, and the Caribbean scuttlebutt. The locals "soft you with a smile" and before you know it, you're taking up their gentle manner, relaxed dress, easy attitude, and their favorite pastime—"liming"—simply hanging out and freeing up your spirit by not doing much of anything at all.

Liming is Caribbean slang, a term born in Trinidad that has spread upward throughout the islands. You hear it everywhere: "Where you limin' later?" "Want to go for a little lime?" "You be limin'?" Liming is downtime, with no thought of work or problems, which can be done practically anywhere: during a Friday-night fish fry, on a tire swing hung from an arched palm tree, in the cockpit of a sailboat anchored in a secluded cove.

Probably the most famous limin' spot in the world is a sand-floored beach bar on the isle of Jost Van Dyke: Foxy's Tamarind Bar, run by a barefoot, singing "genuine Caribbean man" who still lives in the house where he was born. Foxy Callwood has created one of the most relaxed, unpretentious spots in the universe, where, at the edge of Great Harbour you can discover and savor what he has dubbed the "true soul food": waters the color of blueberry snow cones, a line of hammocks swinging between coconut palms growing where the sand meets the sea, great barbecue, and little decks shaded by tin roofs, perfect spots to put your feet up and stare mindlessly out across the water, relishing the feeling of doing nothing constructive for hours. It's the ultimate lime.

Island Wise

So yachties make a beeline for this harbor, and travelers come by interisland ferry, because the barefoot man makes it so easy to shift into island-style idling: becoming one with the sun, sea, and sand—becoming one with our own barefoot spirit.

Even though idling has gotten a bad rap on the mainland (heaven forbid we indulge too much in lackadaisical moments), in-the-know world travelers and yachtsmen find their way to Foxy's when life starts feeling too heavy and hectic because they recognize him as the guru of changing mainstream attitudes—the subject of the songs he makes up and sings to those who seek his wisdom.

"I enjoy life every day that comes," Foxy says, his gentle eyes dancing with amusement at life. "I take that fun and pass it to others so they can smile, relax, and enjoy their days. A few drinks, listenin' to me sing, gettin' in the hammocks and hearin' the waves and wind in the palm trees—it's soul food." He has wise words for those who scoff at downtime as he slides up on his old wooden stool and starts an easy strum of his guitar. "Don't think you're holding up the whole world. If you drop dead, the world will keep going. What the hell do you think you're doing? Enjoy! Enjoy every day!

"Too many strings," he sings, "attached to mainland life. Across the ocean lies a beautiful island, lots of time for sailing and walking barefoot in the sand. Enjoy yourself, it's later than you think."

His songs ring true; the melody and messages will play over

and over in a traveler's mind for months, even years after he says goodbye to Jost Van Dyke. Most who come here experience a transformation: fidgety hands grow still, whirling minds find peace, long-lost dreams surface, and love for and leniency with ourselves and others surge from a deeper place. We begin to re-feel life.

When we finally sail off to the next island, we feel lighter: a leather cord strung with seashells has replaced the heaviness of gold around the neck, undies and an oversized tank top have become the uniform of sailing days, and the fridge is stocked with bottles of Carib beer, which we all hold up to the sunny sky, vowing to return to limin' times at Foxy's.

LIME AID

These days many of us feel that we are lacking the steadiness, stability, and balance our life needs. We pray for better coping skills, ask for more suitable solutions, long for a more logical world, and pray for a reprieve, a chance to recharge. But many mainlanders view idling as taboo, as worthless because, in their view of life, our time is worthless if nothing is being accomplished. We view those who partake in idle moments as misguided. But in actuality, by letting ourselves lime we are merely taking care of ourselves.

To lime is to grant ourselves a great favor; it is an act of kindness toward ourselves, a show of respect toward our health, a courtesy to our spirit. We become, in sailor lingo, "becalmed"— that state when the wind has ceased pushing us and we're just quietly drifting with the current into long-forgotten inner and outer places. It empowers us to be better, to make the most of what comes our way, to be more creative with our perceptions. We begin to think fun thoughts; it's easier to laugh, to be nice, to love; it's easier to cope with life and, thus, make the most of it.

English clergyman and author Robert Burton once said, "Idleness is an appendix to nobility." I interpret these words to mean that liming is an adjunct, not to royalty but to the nobleness of living honestly and authentically. Idling allows us to relax, realign, and rebalance ourselves physically, mentally, and spiritually; it's a luxury wherein we strive for nothing, we do not have to please anyone or take on obligation. It's a chance to simply be—free of charge.

Vacations were originally meant to be great times of idleness: lazing in the sun on an island beach, feeling all of the freeing sensations of the tropics, or chilling out in a cozy little mountain retreat connecting with self and nature. But vacations, too, have become a "go, go, go" affair: twenty-six countries in twenty-seven days, or seeing every museum and attraction in a city over a long weekend. We're always on the move, connecting only on a surface level, without uniting with the true essence of a place, its people, the moment, or ourselves—just as we live out our days back home. We ignore our need to lose ourselves in doodling on golden sands, or simply in enjoying friends. We forget that vacation is meant to be rest for an extended period of time, just as we forget that restful fun is important within our days at home.

If I could, I'd stay anchored in Great Harbour, swinging in a hammock and staring out at the azure waters to the islands of St. Thomas and St. John beyond. But since I can't, I slip into blissful idling at home by doing what I love: sitting alone in a sauna and letting the hot moisture melt away muscle tightness, dancing my way through NIA (Neuromuscular Integrative Action) classes, and taking long bicycle rides at the crack of dawn. These are the things that unstick me when I feel stuck and make my life feel as delicious as one of Foxy's guava coladas. What are yours?

★ *Take a soul siesta.* Personal downtime is a thera-peutic siesta for the soul when its done with playful, islandy charm: find open space and fly a kite, blow bubbles in the backyard and watch them float on the breeze, catnap, sunbathe in a chaise lounge with the sprinkler cooling you down, go sledding on your favorite hill early in the morning before the rest of the world awakes, fingerpaint, putter in a garden, bake a cake—there are a million playful possibili-ties.

Island Wise

★ *Group lime.* Backyard barbecues, pizza parties, girls' nights out. Simple get-togethers with best friends add great joy to our days and relax our thoughts, as long as everyone agrees to the number one limin' rule: no talk about work or problems of any kind. Joke, laugh, reminisce, play games. Simply hang loose and have a light-hearted, liming good time with no thought to cares or woes.

★ *Find your own Foxy.* Discover a Foxy-kind-of-place in your neighborhood, an outdoor cafe where you can relax and people watch. Enjoy the warming familiarity of a local Cheers-type hangout where everybody knows your name, a haunt with a great jukebox whose music can transport you to other great moments in your life. Or simply turn down the lights and turn on the Caribbean tunes of a Jimmy Buffett CD in your own living room—and dream of limin' in the islands.

The Galápagos
Islands, Ecuador

CREATURE COMFORTS

I felt like Alice tumbling into a wonderland of magnificent creatures when I stepped into the Galápagos Islands: a jabbering mockingbird boldly landed atop my sneakers and tugged away at my shoelaces; masked boobies fearlessly walked over to my feet, looked up, held eye contact for a second or two and then, unimpressed, strolled on by; eye-level branches of island scrub held magnificent frigate birds that looked me over with an amused glint in their eyes as they sat contentedly beside their chicks in giant nests.

More masked boobies sat below on ground nests, carefully

rearranging their eggs as we watched, just inches away, and red-footed boobies perched with their Santa-bright webbed feet curled around low-lying limbs. As we walked along the paths brightened by sunny yellow flowers, we all treaded ever-so-carefully to avoid stepping on the sweet Galápagos doves who had no notion of moving as we approached. And this was just an initial ten-minute taste of life in this pristine archipelago that straddles the equator six hundred miles off the coast of Ecuador.

Some mornings we awoke to large pods of dolphins leaping alongside the boat or showy humpback whales breaching and spyglassing, seemingly as curious about us as we were about them. At night we toasted the marvels of nature with cocktails on the open-air deck of our mini–cruise ship, where the stars of the Southern Cross flickered above the jet-black sky like big, perfectly cut diamonds. Encounters on these remote islands—one of the world's most valuable living laboratories—transform lives by gifting us with a better understanding of the earth's creatures, thus improving our relationship with all the inhabitants of our small planet. Since we, as human beings, are the intruders in this wild place, I felt privileged to witness the power of nature here, as well as its inherent capacity for harmony and peace.

The islands were made famous in the 1800s when a young, controversial scientist named Charles Darwin came calling and was blown away by the "divergent characteristics" of the islands' animals. In 1936 Ecuador began actively protecting the flora and fauna, and later the Charles Darwin Research Station and

UNESCO passed laws to guard the islands' species. Today, the islands are a protected World Heritage Site, and only a limited number of island sites are open to a small number of visitors each year (naturalists accompany them to ensure that they behave themselves on their explorations).

Orlando and Reynata were the animal-loving, eco-minded naturalists who escorted us, twice a day, from the ship into *pangas* and motored us to amazing locales, all framed by the islands' haunting volcanic beauty. And talk about wild things! Families of sea lions lounged on the snow-white coral sands of Darwin Bay, scores of pups nursing contentedly from their mothers. Hundreds of marine iguanas lay on coal-black lava fields, soaking up the sun, lava lizards scurried about, and scarlet-and-yellow Sally Lightfoot crabs, one of the world's prettiest crustaceans, loafed near the waterline.

Twelve thousand pairs of huge-winged albatross that have settled in on the isle of Española were enormously entertaining, performing their courtship rituals, tending their extralarge eggs, and, after waddling down the path right on our heels, lining up like jets taking off at a busy airport, launching themselves into the air's currents, and fully extending their six-and-a-half-foot wingspans. Red-billed tropic birds, considered among the most beautiful in the world, flew out from secreted niches in the high, rocky cliffs, their extralong, graceful white tails streaming against a fiercely blue sky.

Later, we snorkeled off the shore of other islands where marine iguanas dove to munch on sea algae, brilliant red-orange octopi glided through a rainbow-mix of tropical fish and the best playmates of all, the sea lions, dove in and joined the fun, whirling and twirling at lightning-fast speed, lightly brushing against me, coming face-to-face to peer into my eyes, then blowing a wall of bubbles and vanishing in a flash.

This kind of contact with the earth's creatures is important for all of us to have, as it allows us to cultivate a deeper reverence for life on earth, a richer appreciation of the gifts of each and every species, a deeper empathy for Mother Earth's sorrowful loss of habitat, and a rock-solid determination to better protect our environment and its inhabitants. The creatures of the world make life more beautiful, more entertaining, more joyous, and bless us with a better understanding of ourselves.

ANIMAL MAGNETISM

Creatures comfort us, whether they be fireflies lighting up the night, a koala bear snuggled up in a tree, or a kitten contentedly purring in our lap. They add warm, fuzzy feelings to our days, often prompt an internal grin, calm us down, and make the greatest of companions. As novelist George Eliot reminds us, "Animals are such agreeable friends—they ask no questions, they pass no criticism."

Island Wise

Critters can be our best therapy. It has been scientifically proven that just stroking a purring cat or contented little ball of puppy fur can lower blood pressure, ease us into relaxation, and wrap us in the calming solace of feeling that we're never really alone. So mingling with animals, whether they're out in nature or within the warmth of our own homes, can work miracles in our lives, strengthening our hearts, our health, and our emotional well-being.

No one can deny that a day starts off on a more enchanting note when we open our door to the seductive call of a loon, a wide-eyed deer poised in the backyard, a turtle moseying on by, or a even tropical lizard boldly sitting on a banana leaf, enjoying the morning breeze. Or, indoors, when we encounter a pair of canaries singing their hearts out, a goldfish swimming to the top of the bowl as we approach, or kisses from a wagging-tailed dog—a display of pure joy and devotion that tells us no one else in the world loves us so unconditionally. What would our days be like without the inspiration of our precious friends?

Connecting with that tenderness of spirit in the Galápagos Islands inspired me to look in my own backyard for opportunities to get more acquainted with animals of the wild. I answered a call for round-the-clock volunteers to care for a gravely ill pygmy sperm whale who had beached himself in nearby shallows. I donned my wet suit, quietly slipped into his tank, and when I slid my hand underneath him, my perception of the wild world changed: I felt the heartbeat of a gentle creature I had long admired from afar, and it beat in the same rhythm as mine. I looked into his gentle eyes and felt as if I saw his soul—his pain, his sadness, his loss of hope, and his fear.

The whale passed away on Christmas Day and everyone who had been touched by the sweet-tempered creature grieved. He had quickly gained the love and respect of everyone who came into contact with him, calmly accepting the best of what we had to give, but in actuality, he gave us much more than he received. This closest of encounters moved me to support those, like ethologist Jane Goodall or the late primatologist Dian Fossey, who believe in the emotional soul and powerful intellect of animals.

I learned that if we let them, animals speak to our spirits and our spirits speak back, fostering an unusual, extraordinary understanding, that, if we open up to it, has the power to make our world a better place for all of us to live.

✳ *Make your yard into an animal playground.* Trade in manicured lawns for front- and backyard habitats planted for wildlife. Create the perfect habitat for critters in need: plant closely spaced fruit or nut-producing shrubs, flowers for butterflies and hummingbirds, water to lure ducks, frogs, and dragonflies. Or a pond for fish, nest boxes for blue-birds, birdbaths and feeders. For more ideas, try www.wildlifegardening.com, or call 703-438-6000 for the National Wildlife Federation's Backyard Wildlife Habitat Program.

✮ *Engaging critters.* Schedule time to horseback ride in the country or at the shore, head to your state parks at sunrise or sunset when the critters are out feeding, walk a neighbor's dog, spend the day at a butterfly garden, or go snorkeling. Discover what creatures tug most at your heart and acquaint yourself with them in an intimate way.

✮ *Get your animal "degree."* Check out the Humane Society University, a program offered by The Humane Society of the United States, to "enrich [your] understanding of animals, human-animal interactions, and humane/environment issues" (www.humanesocietyU.org).

✮ *Stand up for our animal friends.* Join in the fun of actively protecting the sea turtles, bald eagles, whales, chipmunks, or hedgehogs of your area; donate time at your local bird rehab; train your dog or cat to cheer up hospital or nursing home patients:

The possibilities are endless. Team up with one of the activist groups that rally for habitat preservation in not only your own community, but all over the world, like the World Wildlife Fund (www.wwf.org) or the National Audubon Society (www.audubon.org).

St. Lucia

SAVOR THE FLAVORS

The air in St. Lucia seems to sing out in lively Creole patois, the rhythm of reggae gets the body movin', and the coastal road to Soufrière, "the bread basket" of the island, is thrill-filled with twisting, turning hairpin curves that wind into the ear-popping heights of the mountains. The panoramas along the way are dramatic montages of sky-kissing peaks and sea-deep valleys carpeted in cocoa trees and banana plantations. The edge of the rain forest meets the road, seductive in its glimpses of what lies within the interior—tree ferns growing wild and tall, plunging waterfalls, and elephant ears so big they're plucked and used as umbrellas by locals caught in summer showers. Nutmeg, calabash, and cashew trees are impressively laden with fruits, and off in the distance eye-catching outbursts of dense white steam rising from fumaroles and pools of boiling water signal the life of the Soufrière volcano smoldering deep within this independent Caribbean island.

Along the way, travelers can catch a glimpse of the life of the islanders: cassava bread stands line the roads, traditionally baking this island staple with a piece of banana leaf protectively lain between the heavy, pancake-shaped dough and its hot baking surface. Some of the village women who prefer to bring their laundry to the Canaries River stand barefoot with their friends in the cool, clean waters, talking and laughing as they hand-scrub, rinse, and spread their clothes out on warm rocks to dry under the intense blue sky. Men, women, and children stroll up and down hilly lanes in the perfect posture of an unhurried stride, balancing everything from hulking stalks of bananas to sacks of pigeon peas on their heads.

It's easy to see that agriculture is the lifeline of the island: the banana boat arrives in the harbor every Thursday and departs loaded down, its course set for Europe; cocoa is shipped out to Hershey, Pennsylvania, and other harvests include everything from over one hundred identified varieties of mangos to cut tropical flowers used in hotel lobbies and restaurants. The crops planted on family land handed down through generations are worked with simple hoes and "forks," while trees bearing the likes of breadfruit and coconut are climbed barefoot ("You can't climb a tree with shoes on!" one local exclaimed) and harvested with machetes. The country people of St. Lucia are unafraid of manual labor; in fact, they seem to thrive on it, reaping the benefits of physically fit–looking bodies, glowing skin, impressive carriage, and extremely friendly dispositions.

They remain loyal to many of the old island ways, especially when it comes to farming, cooking, and eating. It's a healthy lifestyle, rising at the crack of dawn, walking to the farm, and "pushing the work" to get the produce to the markets on time. They're proud that they burn more calories than local office workers, that the air they breathe is clean and fresh, and that there are "less fat problems" because they eat their "own grown" vegetables and fruit, home cooked, in the traditional ways of their forebears, on small clay coal-pots fired up in the bright orange heat of charcoal (oftentimes, still handmade).

"I guess we're into slow food here," one local told me. "Anything that's cooked nice and slow on a coal pot tastes so much better than stove cooking. Flavor is still very important to St. Lucians; it's still a part of enjoyin' the day!"

Even the islanders with modern kitchens, whether in the country or city, look forward to going out under a nice tree in the yard, sitting in the shade, and getting the charcoal burning. When the fire's glow is just right, a clay or modern metal pot or pan is filled with fresh ingredients and put right on top of the glowing coals.

"If you cook on a regular stove in the kitchen," a local woman said, "we call it 'pre-cooking' the food because it cooks so fast you lose the flavors. The coal pot cooks so nice and slow [like the rhythm of life on the island] and brings out all of the wonderful flavors. It allows for spices, like our local salt, mace, nutmeg, hot peppers, rosemary, celery, and onions to marry. They really need that time, you know, to let go of their flavors and to blend with each other."

So I delighted in the savory mealtime aromas embracing the island with the scent of bread or simple yellow egg cakes baking atop a coal pot, or a vegetable-and-spice-laden fish broth leisurely simmering. Often there's more than one coal pot burning at a time; a chicken, accented with fresh herbs, may be slow-stewing on one while another tranquilly cooks Irish potatoes, water, onion, parsley, garlic, pumpkin, and ground provisions like dasheen, yams, or the giant-sized carrots they raise. When both are done, they're joined on a platter, offering an unexcelled mixture of fall-off-the-bone tenderness and tantalizing flavors that linger in the mind long after the meal has ended.

The islanders take their time savoring the results, too, enjoying one of the greatest side benefits of home cooking—family meal time. Everyone gathers together to thoroughly enjoy the exciting, palatable flavors of their island, with the people they love.

Island Wise

A MATTER OF TASTE

St. Lucians have made zesty flavors a priority in their days. They take their time to pick selectively from their fields or gardens or to shop the produce stands for the highest-quality ingredients, preparing them simply and cooking them oh-so-slowly, mixing in pride, love for self, family, and health, and a great appreciation for flavorful pleasures.

But slow food, and all of its wonderful sensations and rewards, seems to be rapidly vanishing on the mainland, replaced by less than delectable fast food. The experts tell us that nowadays, even with all of our fancy kitchens, we're more at a loss in cooking at home than at any other time in our history. The usual rhetoric is "We don't have time." Translation: It's simply not a priority.

So instead of cooking from the heart, we fill up on fast food, either using up our time driving to chain restaurants only to wait in line for greasy burgers and fries, or filling our freezers and cupboards with expensive processed and packaged food whose taste is comparable to cardboard, plastic, and chemicals. And everything is compounded by sugars, fats, and artificial flavorings. We toss food into a microwave, nuke it to semiconsciousness, and eat: a nutritiously questionable and barely pleasureable way to dine. No wonder we've lost interest in the kitchen and eating at home.

Sometimes the easiest food is the best, like a fresh crunchy salad served with a simple pasta, or a piece of fish drizzled in a little olive oil grilled with an ear of sweet corn, a pork chop placed under the broiler paired with steamed broccoli, or home-made burgers topped with lettuce, tomatoes, pickles, and a bun grilled for a few seconds for an extra-loving touch. Savoring flavors, textures, and aromas doesn't require an evening of preparation.

When we welcome slow food into our homes, we invoke a powerful presence, for food has a soul that, when treated honorably, treats our senses honorably in return. When allowed to cook in its own tranquil time in our own kitchens, slow-cooked food blesses us with some of life's greatest pleasures: alluring, exciting flavors that arouse and tantalize our taste buds so much that we look forward to meals instead of viewing them as a bore and a chore; a house overflowing in comforting, caring scents from cinnamon and rosemary to garlicky chicken soup and tangy barbecue sauce; and a greater sense of community and family, safety and security when dining with others.

For what could be better than preparing dinner and gathering around the table, TV turned off and telephone muted, and offering thanks for being together to enjoy these home-cooked simple pleasures. It's a ritual that lends a protective constancy to our lives, a comforting guarantee that no matter what our age, there's special time set aside every day just to share with those we care about, to talk and be heard, to assess each other's problems and help if we can, to relish each other's delights and, most important, to keep us familiar as we grow from one phase of life into another. As Italian cookbook author Marcella Hazan reminded me, "Good food is the one thing we all have in common," no matter what stage of life we may be passing through.

☆ *Learn to use a slow cooker*. Once known as a Crock-Pot, this wonderful addition to the kitchen is our own version of the St. Lucian clay coal-pot. You can set chicken and veggies to lazily cook while you're at work, permitting island time to gradually infuse the dish with extra-tender qualities and blend mouth-watering flavors. It's ready to serve when you get home—easy, tasty, and a joy to eat.

☆ *Double up*. Make double batches of pasta sauces, soups, stews, cookies, lasagnas, chilies, etc. and store the extra ones in the freezer for flavorful, yet easy warm-ups on those extra-busy nights when you may be tempted into fast food. Never underestimate the flavor of leftovers—oftentimes they're better the second, or third, time around.

☆ *Kitchen timer*. Get real about the amount of time you spend driving to a restaurant, waiting for a table, ordering, and waiting for your food. Chances are you could have cooked something in less time, and with less expense, in your own home. Add up the hours you spend eating out in one week and then, as an experiment, spend them in your own kitchen the next.

★ *Release your kitchen spirit.* With a positive attitude toward getting back to flavorful cooking, working with ingredients our earth naturally provides, and reaping the benefits of home cooking, your time in the kitchen can leave you with a calm, satisfied feeling. Many people find simple cooking simply relaxing.

Sjælland, Denmark

✳

RECLAIM YOUR HOLIDAY SPIRIT

*W*intertime in Copenhagen, Denmark's capital on the island of Sjælland, is warmed by the golden glow of *hygge* (pronounced hue-gah): a comforting coziness the Danes create with millions of candle flames dancing in windows, entryways, and on tables everywhere you look.

Hygge is the crowning touch to an already enchanting city, which seems as if it's been lifted right out of a children's picture book: ancient castle-styled buildings crowned in ornate copper roofs turned green by the elements of passing centuries; fantasy-like spires reaching for the heavens; timeworn cobblestone streets filled with lighthearted city dwellers riding bicycles to and from work; and a dearly loved queen residing royally in an old-world palace. This is the stunning vision that inspired the imaginative tales of master storyteller Hans Christian Andersen, who himself wrote that the relaxed, unpretentious Christmas season here was "quite unforgettably magnificent."

The Danes are completely in love with, and eagerly anticipate, the more than monthlong celebration that woos and wows the playful, yet spiritual, souls of Danish adults as much as it does the children's. Christmas is celebrated to the hilt, and the heart has forever been the country's symbol for this season. Bright-red hearts are everywhere, from the centers of real evergreen garlands stretching across Strøget, the city's famous pedestrian shopping avenue, to big heart-shaped suckers inscribed with "*Glædelig Jul,*" Danish for Merry Christmas. And, of course, they adorn the city's trees. Even the most modern of Copenhageners find continued joy in traditions practiced for over two hundred years: rice pudding with hidden lucky almonds, hand-painted marzipan pigs, which bring good fortune, the sociable warmth of *glögg* (spiced and steamy red wine) and *æbleskiver* (addictively delicious dumplings dipped in bowls of powdered sugar and strawberry jam).

Every year Tivoli Gardens (the world's oldest amusement park) hosts the Royal Danish Ballet's classical performance of *The Nutcracker.* Gingersnaps and roast goose stuffed with apples and prunes are enjoyed throughout the island. Almost every branch of fresh-cut fir trees magically glitters in the fireglow of real candles, and all the children and adults hold hands and play-fully dance round and round the tree singing traditional carols. The Danish also nurture a strong belief in *Julemanden,* Father Christmas, and grumpy, mischievous gnomes called *nisser,* who hide out in attics or barn lofts and love to play practical jokes on everyone. Children set out bowls of porridge for them on Christ-mas Eve, the day to gain their favor, and thus ensure good fortune for the coming year.

While the children hang stockings every night from the first through the twenty-fourth of December and awake each morning to little gifts, adults plunge into the festivities with three to four "Christmas lunches" a week, each traditionally lasting for hours and hours, even on workdays. It's relaxed merriment at its finest, made even more special when feasting in a Tivoli restaurant like the typically Danish Grøsten. The shimmer of candlelight ac-companies the crowds' hearty laughter and cheers of "*Skôl!*" as big glasses of specially brewed "Christmas beer" raised in merry toasts. Guests partake in the pairing of aquavit and herring, dine on the famous Yuletide smørrebrød (open-faced sandwiches of dark, buttered rye bread topped with everything from pork to smoked salmon), and take in the mystical view of thousands of twinkle lights adding enchantment to the Nisse village and ice skaters on Tivoli Lake. The experience resurrects the magic of the season within even the most hardened of hearts, for these are the types of spiritual banquets that stir up every kind of holiday sentiment, no matter what your heritage or beliefs.

The Danes' passion for celebration is alive within their intimate home gatherings, too, like the one I relished in a magical-looking eighteenth-century building right next door to where Hans Christian Andersen once lived in the historic canal district of Nyhavn. Old-fashioned candlelit lanterns guided the way to the top of a curving staircase where the door opened on to a room bathed in the perfumes of the season—pine, oranges, and cloves—and a fresh tree lit by the flickering flames of white candles, trimmed in traditional handmade paper ornaments of cones and hearts shaped into pockets for holding little goodies, topped by a star (the only treetop decoration used in Denmark). The windowsills held baskets of walnuts, hazelnuts, oranges, and apples, and thick red candles sat encircled by fresh evergreen wreathes.

The warmth, the fun, the reverence of seasonal sentiment embraced us all as we gathered around a large table, creating a feeling of family even though some of us had never met before. We talked, cut and wove shiny red-and-white paper hearts to hang on the tree, passed trays of luscious homemade Danish cookies, and lingered over steamy mugs of *glögg* served with pretty silver spoons for scooping out the wine-soaked raisins and slivered almonds at the bottom.

Later on, the room grew still and we all felt Andersen's spirit fill the room as Gita, our host, read us "The Little Match Girl." When I left, I marveled at how the island's simple traditions and the Danes' unbridled enthusiasm had revealed the true essence and nurturing nature of our holiday seasons in a way that I had never experienced before. Whether you celebrate Chanukah, Kwanzaa, or Christmas, the winter holidays and the spirit they invoke invite us to reflect on everyday miracles and open ourselves to shared warmth and joy.

CELEBRATE SINCERELY

For most of us, no matter what our religion or ancestry, December is a hectic month filled with the stresses of overcommitment (of time, money, and energy) and overdoing, outdoing, and pleasing others. The result: "Scrooge-atude," a lost enthusiasm because we perceive the season to be playing havoc with our finances, the balance of family life, and our sanity. We forget that it was designed to be a sacred time that reminds us of how we should live the whole year round—when we treat others with extra kindness, remember to value tradition, friends, and family, listen to music, dance and laugh together, worship and commemorate our individual beliefs, and take time off from work to enjoy it all. That's why they're called "the holidays." They're meant to be restful, relaxed times, away from drudgery, toil, and tension, so that our spirits can rejuvenate.

But it's hard to rest and relax when we're caught up in the "present trap" of out-of-control gift-giving and spending; it has a knack for blowing the worthwhile sentiments right out of our holidays, no matter which ones we observe.

My own holiday spirit suffered a blow when I came home from a wonderful pre-Christmas trip to a Bahamian island where the holidays, and preparation for their December 26 Junkanoo celebration, were being carried out with island-style simplicity. Kids were painting Styrofoam buoy balls to present to their parents, women were baking breads and cakes, and everyone was sewing lively-colored costumes and polishing up their cowbells for the Junkanoo parade. I could just feel the spirit of the season in the air—it was warm, genuine, and all-encompassing just like in Copenhagen. But I arrived back in Florida to find parents grabbing, fighting, and knocking each other down in stores to get the "in" toy of the year and paying exorbitant prices on the Internet "black market" for, well, a toy. I felt sick at heart, and longed to recapture the holiday atmosphere of the islands.

The good news is, as the Danes show us, it is possible to relax into the mood and reinsert the "happy" into our Chanukahs, put the "merry" back into our Christmases, and keep the African-American spirit of family and harvest in our Kwanzaas. We can resurrect the true meaning of these occasions and observances and bring magic and fun into our lives without the tension, fatigue, and worry that seem to be expected as part of the modern holiday season. It's simply a matter of exercising our right to choose, and to change, our mindsets and habits, to listen to our heart's desires and let them guide the way to celebrating our special seasons simply, easily, and with love. We can elect to, as one Dane put it, "do what we like and keep it down-to-earth."

A fun and easy way to step back into the authenticity of any holiday is to light up the room in the warmth of *hygge*, whip up a pitcher of hot *glögg*, a big bowl of popcorn, and gather everyone to watch the classic film *It's a Wonderful Life*. This December tradition reminds us of what both the season and, ultimately, life is really all about: anchoring ourselves through affection, compassion, gratitude, friendship, and, yes, believing in the guidance of "guardian angels." This is the formula for contributing toward peace and goodwill all over the earth, all of the time—and a blueprint for celebrating life the whole year through.

* *Celebrate the season your way.* Gather your family, discuss alternatives, and decide together to be courageous enough to celebrate in your own heartfelt way, setting your sights on stress-free, joyful grins, home and hearth, and sincerity of spirit. Look for the hidden treasures within the holiday season you won't find in any store.

* *Choose gifts from the heart.* Give from your heart. Instead of buying gifts, write letters, poems, or sto-

ries. Or make scrapbooks or collages that express your love and gratitude, and evoke memories of your family and friends. Wrap them up in big red bows. They'll be cherished forever and mean much more than a store-bought gift.

★ *Be charitable.* Give to a loved one's favorite charity in that person's name, gather toys for migrant or homeless children, bake cookies for a child development center or a nursing home, or read books to ill children in hospitals. You can continue to spread holiday spirit all year through by brightening the days of others.

★ *Simply cut back.* Remember that what decorations go up, must come down, that what gets spent must be paid, and that what is given as a gift isn't always used. Keep it sweet and simple.

Seguin Island, Maine

※

TREASURE TENDING TO
HEARTH AND HOME

In an enchanting little cove cradled between the rocky cliffs of Seguin Island, we secured our boat on a mooring, dinghied ashore, and were welcomed by the summer lighthouse keepers, the isle's only human inhabitants. The young couple instructed us on timing the waves to safely step onto the boulder-strewn shore, then led us up a steep path of foot-trampled grass paralleled by the weather-beaten wooden tracks of an antique tramway car. In its prime, and with the aid of oxen, it had hauled lightkeepers of another time, their families, and supplies

186 feet above sea level to the Seguin Island Light Station, the highest elevated light in the State of Maine.

When we reached the top, the sky was a clear and celestial blue, the air tinged in a maritime mixture of sea salt, a hint of seaweed, the sweetness of flowering berry bushes, and the fresh scent of just-mowed grass. There was a heavenly quiet, save for the never-ending echo of hefty waves crashing ashore far below and the lighthearted songs of purple martins that had settled in at the "martin motel," the caretakers' only neighbors for many watery miles.

A mystical, other-world aura prevailed, that sense of being watched over by the spirits of so many who had lived here for over two hundred years, ever since George Washington himself commissioned the historic lighthouse in 1795. It was here on Seguin Island that I rediscovered the little pleasures hidden within life's simple chores.

I must admit, I was a bit envious of the caretakers who had volunteered for the summer to care for one of our nation's grandest old dames of seafaring history. They were dropping out of their normal lives to rediscover all the wonderful delights of living simply. They plunged right in, having fun prettying up the place by filling the old window boxes of the caretaker's cottage with brilliant red geraniums; mowing fast-growing grasses while savoring their clean, summery smells; and planting (with pride) their first-ever vegetable garden on the protected leeward side of the granite tower, rigging it with chicken wire and colorful lobster buoys gone astray to keep the island's rabbits from munching the fruits of their labor.

They discovered the delight of plucking berries right off the bushes, feeding the birds, and keeping the lighthouse windows clean as a whistle. Within their peaceful isolation they conserved water, cooked simply, talked more to each other, and never tired of watching the silvery light of the beacon protectively scan the surrounding waters, still, after centuries, guiding sea captains to safety.

As they unlocked the door to the tower and we started the climb to the top, it took only a touch of imagination to hear the echoing footsteps of the old keepers who climbed the circular staircase night after night to keep the flame burning. Today it's automated, but ducking outside onto the gallery (the light's circular balcony), we felt so high and so far away from the rest of the world that it seemed we were the only people on earth.

Later we all lazed on the grass in a companionable silence, transported back to another type of life—distant, yet vaguely familiar, lusciously soul-satisfying, and so simply in sync that time ceased to matter. We savored the calm, the view, the quaint pleasures of sandwiches, snappy red apples, and chewy oatmeal cookies—all just a little taste of the life held sacred by the "year-rounders" who live on the islands scattered off the coastline of Maine.

These isles have long lured those of hardy, self-reliant stock who relish their little worlds of detached, isolated beauty, independence, calmness, and quiet. They embrace a lifestyle of earlier days, living in accordance with the seasons and working doggedly hard but not minding it one bit. They are dedicated to the good of their community and are determined to nurture and protect the island children and their multigrade one-room schoolhouses. These schools, the island residents will tell you, excel "where mainland schools have missed the mark." Enviable small teacher-student ratios mean children receive individualized attention, have a higher rate of college attendance and completion, and, on average, higher scores on college entrance exams.

These locals typically make their living from the sea, often with family chipping in. And even though they rise in the predawn to start a physically demanding day—hauling lobster, fishing, selling their catch, and maintaining their boats and equipment—time is always found to polish the island fire truck, show up at school functions, help kids with homework, meet friends at sewing circles, open up the post office, and cut flowers from backyard gardens to sell as bouquets in the mom-and-pop grocery stores. And there's always a steamy pot of lobster stew cooking on the stove whose recipe has been handed down through generations of lobstermen. The islanders' days are sprinkled with those simple everyday chores that fill our lives yet give us a sense of structure, consistency, and belonging.

THE PLEASURES OF PUTTERING

There's something remarkably soothing and nurturing about carrying out those tasks that feather our nests and make our life feel grounded and secure. But many of us these days have lost this positive link because we view them as drudgery, as thankless toil, as a boring burden on our precious time.

But as with everything in life, attitude makes all the difference. I know firsthand; as soon as I changed the word "housekeeping" to "homekeeping" my perception of carrying out tasks at home changed. I looked upon them, not as an obligatory cleaning of a structure, but as caring for the place that cradles me and my husband. Thus, I felt like I was attending to my own spirit, as well as to those I love.

Homekeeping invites us to establish a true relationship with the intimacies of the place we call home. It involves finding joy in creating and maintaining those special vibes that ensure that when we enter our home territory we experience warmth, pride, and comfort. It is about raking leaves; helping our kids with homework; keeping the car up and running; planting flowers that suit our spirit; helping our spouses when they need it; preparing hot, healthy breakfasts; making sure everyone has fresh, clean sheets; and covering the walls in family artwork. Homekeeping also translates beyond the front door to the larger community: volunteering to help others, keeping a watch over the land, participating in local government and events, being there for school plays, or forming a neighborhood watch—and discovering a safe haven for the soul in doing it.

For some, discovering the pleasures of homekeeping is a journey back to what either has been forgotten or what has become trivialized by pop culture. For others, it's a step into brand new territory. But for everyone, it can help us reconnect with the basics of good living and the things we value.

Finding little delights within life's sustaining duties requires us to slow down and venture back to a time when people found a spark of fulfillment in daily chores. For example, in dusting our framed photographs, we're offered opportunities to reacquaint ourselves with loved ones and with special moments of the past frozen in time; in taking a feather duster to our knickknacks, we're blessed with time to linger and reconnect with special memories that otherwise too often go forgotten. We can discover that a meditative calmness comes from kneading bread dough or cutting cookies, and our minds are free to wander to higher places in the downtime of washing windows. Problems often find solutions when we engage in automatic activities like vacuuming, and stress and tension get worked out when we mow grass and weed gardens. Puttering is a wonderful, relaxing way of getting things done, but freeing ourselves at the same time. Sometimes all you need to do is set the scene: put on some rock and roll and dance across the patio with a broom; don a bathing suit and sun your-self while gardening; discover the easy tranquillity of cutting veg-etables and stirring them into a homemade minestrone. I love *not* handing these little tasks off to other people to take care of—and that's a brand new attitude, courtesy of the year-rounders on the islands of Maine.

* *Make it fun!* Before you psych yourself *out* of your little chores, cop your own new attitude. Make it fun! Pour a glass of wine, turn on the music, grab the dust rag, the iron, or vacuum and go to town. Tak-ing care of your own things may be the only time you are intimately in touch with them.

* *Get your hands dirty.* Head to the country for an afternoon of picking your own apples, green beans, strawberries, tomatoes, blueberries. Go home, sit down under a tree or on your porch swing and snap the beans, shuck the peas, peel the potatoes. It just feels so old-fashioned good!

* *Clear the clutter.* Clutter dampens the beauty and spirit of any home, so clear out anything you haven't used or worn in a year, from hoarded panty hose with runs in them and holey T-shirts to half-

full bottles of hair conditioner and old kitchen spices that have outlived their shelf life. Pitch those piles of magazines you've been meaning to read forever, organize your desk, closets, cupboards, and drawers. Remember, a decluttered home equates to a decluttered life.

Bimini, the Bahamas

TAKE THINGS IN STRIDE

One quiet Sunday morning I was strolling along a sea-wall in Bimini, a tiny Bahamian "out island" that lures big-game fishermen from all corners of the globe. I was having that "islandy" kind of fun, looking down through gin-clear waters where schools of yellow-striped grunt, turquoise parrot fish, and magenta-and-gold tropical fish were lazily hovering around a pile of empty queen conch shells. The shells lay there, in an under-water pyramid of sorts, discarded by locals who had extracted their meat, an island staple cooked up as crunchy conch fritters, spicy conch chowder and, my favorite, sweet and tender cracked conch.

As the sunlight rose above a casuarina tree, a flash of hot pink glimmered from beneath the water. I looked closer to discover one of the largest, most brilliant conch shells I had ever seen, tempting me to add it to my seashell collection. But it was totally beyond my reach.

An elderly man, dressed in his Sunday best, walked past me on his way home from church. "See somet'ing pretty down dere?" he asked in a lilting Bahamian accent.

"That conch shell," I said. "I'd love to have it, but I can't figure out how to get down there to get it."

He walked away without comment, returning a few minutes later with a ladder that he stood in the water, propped against the seawall. "Hold dis steady," he said. He rolled up his pant legs and shirt sleeves and descended the rungs, almost falling in as he stretched to hook the shell with a stick. He climbed up and presented me with not only the shell, but with a big smile and glistening eyes.

"Thank you so much," I said.

"No problem, mon," he said as he and his ladder disappeared down the lane. I stood there, my lovely shell dripping cool seawater in my hand, marveling at the ease of attitude in which this man carried out an act of kindness for a total stranger.

"No problem, mon" is more than an islandy phrase known the world over. These three little words epitomize that wonderful ability of islanders to take things in stride. It's their way of saying that whatever needs doing will get done without angst, without hassle, and without injecting pressure or stress into the moment. They simply go with the flow, looking at the here and now as a special "present" all wrapped up in the beauty of the moment.

Taking things in stride is a well-developed trait of most islanders. They arise each morning ready to deal with the reality of what the day brings. They don't wake up expecting a perfect day without problems to solve, delays, or disappointments. Nor do they expect each moment to cater to their individual whims or desires, as life just doesn't work that way.

But because people on islands live cut off from the rest of the world, they're used to problems. Its normal for the mail boat to be held up by rough seas, for orders to miss supply ships coming from the mainland, and for fishing to be inconsistent. The obstacles and hurdles to overcome are not taken as personal assaults on their own agendas. They seldom fly into a rage, create chaos, moan and groan, or make mountains out of sand hills.

Islanders simply say, "No, problem, mon," and just go on with their day, using their energy to complete other tasks like raising children, giving a stranger a helping hand, and making life sweet. They know there's no sense in getting themselves all riled up, elevating blood pressure, and stressing out every inch of their body and mind. Those reactions don't change anything. In fact, they're counterproductive, negatively affecting us and others.

DON'T BREAK YOUR STRIDE

Many mainlanders have a difficult time taking things in stride. We almost seem to be opposed to the natural flow of life, awakening each morning ready for the race, expecting the day to fall into place according to our own plan, hell-bent on immediate gratification around every corner. When things don't go our way, like undisciplined children, we throw tantrums, creating chaos where there was none—and everyone around us feels the brunt of our stress. We walk around like time bombs, filled with anxiety and a prevailing sense of urgency, always on the verge of exploding.

But these reactions only render us losers, for we lose the ability to enjoy the simple things in life, to connect with our inner being, to create good health, and to love with all of our heart. Our "present" moment is all too often anything but a gift, but rather something viewed as an enemy in an overtaxed day. Patience becomes a foreign concept, kindness an afterthought. Chronic stress begins to replace the relaxed state in which we are meant to live. The ability to take things in stride is completely lost.

Islanders know that if something isn't done within an exact moment, the world is not going to end. Mainlanders feel that it will, so they fall into habits of control and manipulation rather than accept the law of the universe—that everyone is where they're supposed to be at a given moment. When a car won't start, it may be a sign to stay put for reasons unknown to us. When someone needs an "unscheduled" helping hand, view it not as an unwanted interruption, but an opportunity for our spirit to extend kindness. When a personal call interrupts work, it may be a reminder to be grateful that we have a loved one who took a moment out of his or her day to say hello—many people don't.

When we're unable to say, "No problem, mon," and just mosey off to the next project or encounter, it affects not only our own perception of life, but it grinds on those around us who have to listen to the fussing and fuming over all that "small stuff"—a waste of time, energy, and thought for all. Sir William Osler summed it up beautifully: "Things cannot always go your way. Learn to accept in silence the minor aggravations, cultivate the gift of taciturnity and consume your own smoke with an extra draught of hard work, so that those about you may not be annoyed with the dust and soot of your complaints." In other words, lighten up; it's not the end of the world.

En-lightening our attitude is extremely important, for the heaviness of the moment influences how we perceive obstacles, how we respond to problems, and how we treat others. When we get bogged down in sleepless nights, negative emotions, and the tolls of tension, our spirit calls out to us to find our Caribbean soul—to enlighten our attitude by adhering to the mantra "no problem, mon" regardless of what latitude we may call home.

We need to relax our rhythms, slow our pace, and pull out

of the race. Those of us who move the quickest seem most unable to handle even the slightest delay or problem. We're always speeding, running red lights, getting infuriated if we have to stop for pedestrians crossing the street, and taking all kinds of chances with our lives and the lives of others. We're sprinting from one place to another, almost out of control, never having enough time to plan, to breathe, to acknowledge that our day is really not overwhelmed in obstacles but, rather, overflowing with great chances for pleasure. We often become the sole obstacle to our own peace, instead of taking a deep breath and just saying, "No problem."

✴ *Get real.* Let's dive into a reality check on how we respond, or overreact, to different situations. Try this: On a scale of one to ten (ten the highest), rate the situation, as well as your reaction. If the situation is a "two," like slowing down at a school crossing on your way to work, but the reaction is rated a "nine" (equivalent to losing a wallet, let's say), you're needlessly tormenting your own body and mind. Your health, the moment, and your mood all suffer for naught.

✴ *Charge up your power source.* When we choose a tight-fisted stress reaction over acceptance and flexibility, our breathing becomes extremely shallow, the cardiovascular system constricts, depriving everything from muscles to the brain of life-giving oxygen. So breathe deeply, in through the nose for a count of three seconds, hold for two, and exhale completely to the count of six. Ah, feeling better.

☆ *Smiles go miles.* They can melt ice, uplift spirits, disarm anger, and give momentary relief to loneliness. So whether you feel like it or not, put on your best, most sincere outward smile and watch the magic happen. Then learn to smile inside—experience that exhilarating lightheartedness that comes from placing a grin in your belly, a happy face in your lungs and throat, and a big ol' smile in each eye and your forehead.

☆ *Pack a spirit-booster kit.* When detained at a red light, delayed in an airport, left hanging on the phone forever, or even while waiting for your dentist, distract yourself from stressing out with a small book of inspirational quotes, a piece of art your toddler colored just for you, hard candies in all your favorite flavors, or a little photo album brimming with frozen moments of loved ones and special places, perhaps even a favorite island spot.

Epilogue

During my island sojourns, I've met islanders who have become not only cherished friends, but also my inspiration to sustain the island wisdom they have imparted to me. They have shown me that the island paradise we all dream about includes, but goes well beyond, the sugar-white sands and never-ending blue skies. True paradise is the feeling that all is right and beautiful within our own little worlds. These islanders are living proof that a genuine sense of well-being is within easy reach of each and every one of us, regardless of where we call home. It's a matter of deciding to follow the callings of our heart, and resolving to make choices that feel right for us.

The experiences that make life feel better will, of course, vary a bit with each individual. But there are certain essential elements that, because of the way we're made, are key to maintaining balance, clear-mindedness, serenity, and the capacity for a sense of humor. Slowing down to island time is the fundamental factor in creating that feeling of good living because we can truly be conscious of our feelings and inner impressions and thus follow through accordingly. Once we establish this base we can then assess what's genuinely important to us—where our individual values lie, what morals and ethics we are determined to live by, what we are willing to accept in, or discard from, our lives.

From the strength of this foundation, we afford ourselves the opportunity to create the space we need, the peace and quiet so vital to self-nurturing, the communal relationships that lend emotional support, and the security of knowing that, no matter what happens, we will never be alone. It's welcoming that "island 'ting," greeting others with a "good day" and a smile, watching over each other, trusting in the kindness of someone else's heart and securing, in return, their faith in the compassion within our own heart. And it's finding joy in generosity.

My island friends believe that a sense of paradise is also synonymous with a sense of contentment—being happy with what we have, focusing on the present moment and taking things in stride, acknowledging and showing gratitude for the little, yet significant, gifts that come our way. They've helped me to realize how satisfying, easy, and delightful life can feel. I am now a student in the art of living with island wisdom in mind. And I firmly believe that by adopting island-wise choices, anyone can find themselves living within that blissful sense of relaxed well-being, and our own daily taste of paradise will not be lost.

Sometimes, as we all know, old habits try to creep back in and take over. So when mainland frenzy starts to whisk me off course, I just hear the soft, confident voice of one of my Hawaiian friends: "You are an island girl in spirit. You will only find true happiness living as one."

Acknowledgments

✦

Mahalo to the Hawaiian isle of Maui for bringing me together with book editor Dan Smetanka who guided me to the best agent in the world, Paula Balzer of Sarah Lazin Books. I will never be able to thank Paula enough for her inspiration, belief in me, and her love of simpler, island-style living. A big, heartfelt "thank you" is also extended to my editor, Ann Campbell, for her enthusiasm for island life and its wisdom, her vision, and her commitment to quality, and to her wonderful assistant, Jenny Cookson.

My sincerest appreciation goes out to those who gave of themselves and their time so freely: my husband and best friend Darrel Holler, who was always there cheering me on and offering patience, understanding, and lots of tender loving care, my sister, Jacklyn Treneer, my niece Chrystal Treneer, and long-time friend Pam Davidson—who were always available to brainstorm with me no matter what was going on in their lives—and my soul sister Marylou Foley, who introduced me to gentler worlds.

I'm so grateful for the influences of my ever-encouraging mother, Frances Frawley, who has passed on her fun, Hawaiian-loving spirit to me, for my father, who is always there guiding me from beyond, and for all of the amazing islanders I met along this magical journey who shared their hearts and wisdom with me.

ABOUT THE AUTHOR

Janis Frawley-Holler, the travel editor of Florida's award-winning *Sarasota Magazine,* is the author of *Key West Gardens and Their Stories* and is a frequent contributor to *Islands* magazine. Her work has also appeared in *Travel + Leisure, Spa, Family Circle, Cruising World, Sailing World, Gulfshore Life,* and the Michelin travel series. An avid yoga practitioner, she travels extensively and lives in Florida.